ST. LOUIS
REAL ESTATE
INVESTORS
ASSOCIATION

TM

Taking You from  to

Resource Guide

Created by: *John Lee*

STLREIA
St. Louis MO

www.STLREIA.com

STLREIA ~ *Our Purpose*

Real Estate Investing in St. Louis

St. Louis Real Estate Investors Association, Inc.™ STLREIA™ is a non-profit organization dedicated to serving our members. We are the longest active real estate investors association in the St. Louis area.

STLREIA is organized to provide education in the area of real estate investments, to enhance the opportunity for seminar graduates and other members to achieve their individual and financial goals, to promote a spirit of understanding and cooperation between beginning and more experienced investors and to encourage the exchange of ideas between investors.

Price is what you pay. Value is what you get. — Warren Buffett

Contents

Contents

STLREIA Community

St. Louis Real Estate Investors Association™ meets online and offline to bring you the highest value in real estate investing education and many subjects that include world class advice on repairs, marketing, property management and many other topics.

STLREIA features local and nationally known speakers and trainers. We meet live and virtually to promote your real estate investing skills. Being not-for-profit, we strive and focus on what works for you, today.

Our STLREIA community proudly shares networking luncheons in person, as well as online meet ups to converse with fellow investors and learn tricks of the trade, investment strategies, their successes and ways to avoid mistakes. Register for our emails and stay up-to-date with times and locations – visit www.STLREIA.com

Our **Spring Fling** is in April
&
Our **Fall Festival** is in October

Catered Meals – Special Guests – Unbelievable Bonuses

Disclaimer: The St. Louis Real Estate Investors Association does not officially endorse or promote any methods of investing or statements made by persons or organizations that come before the Association to speak. It does not assume any liability for investments or statements of any kind for its members. Association Officers urge all persons to seek advice from qualified and competent professionals.

Board Members

President--Lloyd Alinder

Vice President---Dan Heymann

Treasurer---Ruth Hollander

Secretary--Janet Keller

Membership Chair--Laura Lee

Media Director--Diana Mayo

Past President--Jim Heisserer

Administration Catalyst------------------------------Pat Heisserer

Board Member--Alex Wheatley

Board Member--Laura Jimerson

Program Coordinator--------------------------------------John Lee

Board Member--Jim Choyke

Board Member---Perron Riley

Newsletter Administrator-------------------Grace Waitman Reed

My RE Investment Goals:

"If you don't like where you are, move. You are not a tree." -Jim Rohn

1)_____

2)_____

3)_____

4)_____

5)_____

6)_____

7)_____

8)_____

9)_____

10)_____

January

Stay up~to~date www.**STLREIA**.com

Online

Offline

"Ninety percent of all millionaires become so through owning real estate." -Andrew Carnegie

Notes

February

Stay up~to~date www.STLREIA.com

Online

Offline

"The major fortunes in America have been made in land."
-John D. Rockefeller

Notes

March

Stay up~to~date www.**STLREIA**.com

Online:

Offline:

"Time is more valuable than money. You can get more money, but you cannot get more time."
-John Rohn

Notes

April

Stay up~to~date <u>www.**STLREIA**.com</u>

Online

Offline

"The way we see it, real wealth means having the money and the freedom to live life on your own terms."
Rich Fettke, Co-Founder and Co-CEO of RealWealth

Notes

May

Stay up~to~date www.**STLREIA**.com

Online

Offline

"I would give a thousand furlongs of sea for an acre of barren ground."
-Shakespeare

Notes

June

Stay up~to~date www.STLREIA.com

Online

Offline

"Buying real estate is not only the best way, the quickest way, the safest way, but the only way to become wealthy."
-Marshall Field

Notes

July

Stay up~to~date www.**STLREIA**.com

Online

Offline

"The best investment on Earth is earth."
Louis Glickman, American Business Executive

Notes

August

Stay up~to~date   www.<ins>**STLREIA**</ins>.com

Online

Offline

"Real estate is an imperishable asset, ever increasing in value. It is the most solid security that human ingenuity has devised. It is the basis of all security and about the only indestructible security."
-Russell Sage (August 4, 1816 – July 22, 1906), financier, railroad executive and Whig politician from New York, United States.

Notes

September

Stay up~to~date www.**STLREIA**.com

Online

Offline

"He is not a full man who does not own a piece of land."
-Proverb

Notes

October

Stay up~to~date   www.STLREIA.com

Online

Offline

"Buy land, they're not making it anymore."
-Mark Twain

Notes

November

Stay up~to~date www.**STLREIA**.com

Online

Offline

"Success in real estate starts when you believe you are worthy of it."
-Michael Ferrara

Notes

December

Stay up~to~date www.STLREIA.com

Online

Offline

The Happiest of Holidays to You !!!

"When one door closes, buy another one and open it yourself."
-Anonymous

Notes

"The most important quality for an investor is temperament, not intellect... You need a temperament that neither derives great pleasure from being with the crowd or against the crowd."
-Warren Buffett

Notes

"Buy on the fringe and wait. Buy land near a growing city! Buy real estate when other people want to sell. Hold what you buy!"
-John Jacob Astor

Notes

"Land monopoly is not only monopoly, but it is by far the greatest of monopolies; it is a perpetual monopoly, and it is the mother of all other forms of monopoly."
-Winston Churchill

ST LOUIS REAL ESTATE INVESTORS ASSOCIATION

Stay up~to~date www.STLREIA.com

Idea a Minute

From STLREIA Members

CLEANING:

Drain cleaner: 1 cup baking soda, 1 cup vinegar and a teapot full of hot water to follow.

Flylady.net – has ideas on how to keep your home clean, how to get rid of clutter and has a home maintenance journal.

GENERAL:

For Weeds: 1 gallon vinegar, 1 cup salt, 8 tsp. dish washing soap. Mix and spray on weeds.

Use Kilz on subfloors before laying new pad and carpet.

Use Alive Enzyme to eliminate pet urine.

Use porcelain or ceramic tile. Porcelain is stronger.

Use Behr Deck Over to restore worn out decks (not rotten decks).

Involve your spouse.

HOMES:

To purchase a home: Ask what is the least amount you will take if I buy your home today.

Decide before you buy about how to hold the property (tax implications), how you'll finance it, how you will depreciate it, how to take title.

Landscaping: Evergreen shrubs; variegated yucca plant; crepe myrtle; rose of Sharon; knock out roses; Barberry; yews and Japanese yews; golden euyunomous.

Always have an exit plan when you are purchasing a property.

Choose your "Power team" from those people you trust: Handyman, accountant, attorney, electrician, plumber, insurance agent, banker, etc.

Keep good records. Keep all correspondence.

Always get a building inspection, termite inspection and radon inspection.

Contractors should have workman's comp insurance if they are doing a dangerous job such as tree trimming, roofing, siding etc.

LANDLORDING:

Tenant screening, tenant screening, tenant screening.

Go to the prospective tenant's property to see "how they live".

Don't rent to friends or family.

If you take a tenant that has credit issues: Have employer deposit the rent directly into your bank account.

In lieu of replacing cabinets: Paint cabinets satin black and use brushed nickel knobs.

Utilize craigslist.com and postlets.com (now Zillow rent manager). Make a list of the property descriptions, room dimensions, etc. in Word and then copy and paste to Craigslist/postlets.

Set up Google search for properties and it will alert you if someone else is trying to use your pics/rental home for their own use. Another suggestion was to take the URL link and move it from Postlets to Craigslist and others cannot "steal" your pics.

Rent-o-meter.com: put in a zip code and it will pull up properties in that area and the rents charged.

Send your tenant a bill each month- they are used to getting a bill and will pay a bill.

Create a calendar for tenants i.e.: change furnace filters, change batteries smoke alarm, rent due date.

On your credit application form: put in that you can run credit checks through eternity. (In case you have to collect on judgments)

"Text" tenants rather than calling tenants. The response rate is about 90%.

Use "deposit only" debit cards and give them to your tenants. Bank of America has this program. Your tenants can use the ATM at Bank of America to deposit your rent.

First Community credit Union has "ACH" for free. (Same concept as above drawing your rent money from your tenant's account). This is a free service First Community provides. There is a 1-page application form that your tenant needs to fill in.

Copy the checks you receive from tenants. That way you will have their bank account information.

Advertise before the residence is vacant. Have people waiting and lined up to view the home.

Use casenet.com to check your tenants. To get to website you can Google: casenet in MO

Check on property by having an "exterminator" go through the home on a regular basis.

Use a property manager instead of doing it yourself. Raise the rents by 10% and a property manager won't "cost" you anything.

Security deposit is not your money. Don't comingle funds. Have a separate account for deposit money.

Rent is due on Day 1; it is late on Day 2. Call or text on Day 2.

Show home to multiple prospects at the same time.

Make an effort to get a good tenant rather than settle for a substandard renter just to fill a vacancy.

Always use a tenant screening service. Maintain the yard on vacant properties. When utilizing signs use a stencil with letter large enough to read from the street.

I advise women to invest in real estate. It is the collateral to be preferred above all others, and the safest means of investing money.
-Hetty Green, American Businesswoman and Financier

Protect Your Family From Lead in Your Home

 United States
Environmental
Protection Agency

 United States
Consumer Product
Safety Commission

 United States
Department of Housing
and Urban Development

September 2013

Are You Planning to Buy or Rent a Home Built Before 1978?

Did you know that many homes built before 1978 have **lead-based paint**? Lead from paint, chips, and dust can pose serious health hazards.

Read this entire brochure to learn:

- How lead gets into the body
- About health effects of lead
- What you can do to protect your family
- Where to go for more information

Before renting or buying a pre-1978 home or apartment, federal law requires:

- Sellers must disclose known information on lead-based paint or lead-based paint hazards before selling a house.
- Real estate sales contracts must include a specific warning statement about lead-based paint. Buyers have up to 10 days to check for lead.
- Landlords must disclose known information on lead-based paint and lead-based paint hazards before leases take effect. Leases must include a specific warning statement about lead-based paint.

If undertaking renovations, repairs, or painting (RRP) projects in your pre-1978 home or apartment:

- Read EPA's pamphlet, *The Lead-Safe Certified Guide to Renovate Right,* to learn about the lead-safe work practices that contractors are required to follow when working in your home (see page 12).

Simple Steps to Protect Your Family
from Lead Hazards

If you think your home has lead-based paint:

- Don't try to remove lead-based paint yourself.

- Always keep painted surfaces in good condition to minimize deterioration.

- Get your home checked for lead hazards. Find a certified inspector or risk assessor at epa.gov/lead.

- Talk to your landlord about fixing surfaces with peeling or chipping paint.

- Regularly clean floors, window sills, and other surfaces.

- Take precautions to avoid exposure to lead dust when remodeling.

- When renovating, repairing, or painting, hire only EPA- or state-approved Lead-Safe certified renovation firms.

- Before buying, renting, or renovating your home, have it checked for lead-based paint.

- Consult your health care provider about testing your children for lead. Your pediatrician can check for lead with a simple blood test.

- Wash children's hands, bottles, pacifiers, and toys often.

- Make sure children avoid fatty (or high fat) foods and eat nutritious meals high in iron and calcium.

- Remove shoes or wipe soil off shoes before entering your house.

1

Lead Gets into the Body in Many Ways

Adults and children can get lead into their bodies if they:

- Breathe in lead dust (especially during activities such as renovations, repairs, or painting that disturb painted surfaces).

- Swallow lead dust that has settled on food, food preparation surfaces, and other places.

- Eat paint chips or soil that contains lead.

Lead is especially dangerous to children under the age of 6.

- At this age, children's brains and nervous systems are more sensitive to the damaging effects of lead.

- Children's growing bodies absorb more lead.

- Babies and young children often put their hands and other objects in their mouths. These objects can have lead dust on them.

Women of childbearing age should know that lead is dangerous to a developing fetus.

- Women with a high lead level in their system before or during pregnancy risk exposing the fetus to lead through the placenta during fetal development.

2

Health Effects of Lead

Lead affects the body in many ways. It is important to know that even exposure to low levels of lead can severely harm children.

In children, exposure to lead can cause:

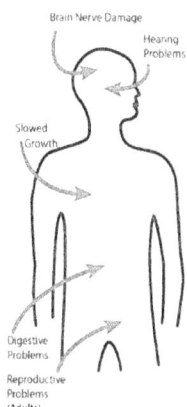

Brain Nerve Damage

Hearing Problems

Slowed Growth

Digestive Problems

Reproductive Problems (Adults)

- Nervous system and kidney damage

- Learning disabilities, attention deficit disorder, and decreased intelligence

- Speech, language, and behavior problems

- Poor muscle coordination

- Decreased muscle and bone growth

- Hearing damage

While low-lead exposure is most common, exposure to high amounts of lead can have devastating effects on children, including seizures, unconsciousness, and, in some cases, death.

Although children are especially susceptible to lead exposure, lead can be dangerous for adults, too.

In adults, exposure to lead can cause:

- Harm to a developing fetus

- Increased chance of high blood pressure during pregnancy

- Fertility problems (in men and women)

- High blood pressure

- Digestive problems

- Nerve disorders

- Memory and concentration problems

- Muscle and joint pain

Check Your Family for Lead

Get your children and home tested if you think your home has lead.

Children's blood lead levels tend to increase rapidly from 6 to 12 months of age, and tend to peak at 18 to 24 months of age.

Consult your doctor for advice on testing your children. A simple blood test can detect lead. Blood lead tests are usually recommended for:

- Children at ages 1 and 2

- Children or other family members who have been exposed to high levels of lead

- Children who should be tested under your state or local health screening plan

Your doctor can explain what the test results mean and if more testing will be needed.

4

Where Lead-Based Paint Is Found

In general, the older your home or childcare facility, the more likely it has lead-based paint.[1]

Many homes, including private, federally-assisted, federally-owned housing, and childcare facilities built before 1978 have lead-based paint. In 1978, the federal government banned consumer uses of lead-containing paint.[2]

Learn how to determine if paint is lead-based paint on page 7.

Lead can be found:

- In homes and childcare facilities in the city, country, or suburbs,

- In private and public single-family homes and apartments,

- On surfaces inside and outside of the house, and

- In soil around a home. (Soil can pick up lead from exterior paint or other sources, such as past use of leaded gas in cars.)

Learn more about where lead is found at epa.gov/lead.

---

[1] "Lead-based paint" is currently defined by the federal government as paint with lead levels greater than or equal to 1.0 milligram per square centimeter (mg/cm), or more than 0.5% by weight.

[2] "Lead-containing paint" is currently defined by the federal government as lead in new dried paint in excess of 90 parts per million (ppm) by weight.

Identifying Lead-Based Paint and Lead-Based Paint Hazards

Deteriorating lead-based paint (peeling, chipping, chalking, cracking, or damaged paint) is a hazard and needs immediate attention. **Lead-based paint** may also be a hazard when found on surfaces that children can chew or that get a lot of wear and tear, such as:

- On windows and window sills

- Doors and door frames

- Stairs, railings, banisters, and porches

Lead-based paint is usually not a hazard if it is in good condition and if it is not on an impact or friction surface like a window.

Lead dust can form when lead-based paint is scraped, sanded, or heated. Lead dust also forms when painted surfaces containing lead bump or rub together. Lead paint chips and dust can get on surfaces and objects that people touch. Settled lead dust can reenter the air when the home is vacuumed or swept, or when people walk through it. EPA currently defines the following levels of lead in dust as hazardous:

- 40 micrograms per square foot ($\mu g/ft^2$) and higher for floors, including carpeted floors

- 250 $\mu g/ft^2$ and higher for interior window sills

Lead in soil can be a hazard when children play in bare soil or when people bring soil into the house on their shoes. EPA currently defines the following levels of lead in soil as hazardous:

- 400 parts per million (ppm) and higher in play areas of bare soil

- 1,200 ppm (average) and higher in bare soil in the remainder of the yard

Remember, lead from paint chips—which you can see—and lead dust—which you may not be able to see—both can be hazards.

The only way to find out if paint, dust, or soil lead hazards exist is to test for them. The next page describes how to do this.

6

Checking Your Home for Lead

You can get your home tested for lead in several different ways:

- A lead-based paint **inspection** tells you if your home has lead-based paint and where it is located. It won't tell you whether your home currently has lead hazards. A trained and certified testing professional, called a lead-based paint inspector, will conduct a paint inspection using methods, such as:

  - Portable x-ray fluorescence (XRF) machine

  - Lab tests of paint samples

- A **risk assessment** tells you if your home currently has any lead hazards from lead in paint, dust, or soil. It also tells you what actions to take to address any hazards. A trained and certified testing professional, called a risk assessor, will:

  - Sample paint that is deteriorated on doors, windows, floors, stairs, and walls

  - Sample dust near painted surfaces and sample bare soil in the yard

  - Get lab tests of paint, dust, and soil samples

- A combination inspection and risk assessment tells you if your home has any lead-based paint and if your home has any lead hazards, and where both are located.

Be sure to read the report provided to you after your inspection or risk assessment is completed, and ask questions about anything you do not understand.

Checking Your Home for Lead, continued

In preparing for renovation, repair, or painting work in a pre-1978 home, Lead-Safe Certified renovators (see page 12) may:

- Take paint chip samples to determine if lead-based paint is present in the area planned for renovation and send them to an EPA-recognized lead lab for analysis. In housing receiving federal assistance, the person collecting these samples must be a certified lead-based paint inspector or risk assessor

- Use EPA-recognized tests kits to determine if lead-based paint is absent (but not in housing receiving federal assistance)

- Presume that lead-based paint is present and use lead-safe work practices

There are state and federal programs in place to ensure that testing is done safely, reliably, and effectively. Contact your state or local agency for more information, visit epa.gov/lead, or call **1-800-424-LEAD (5323)** for a list of contacts in your area.[3]

---

[3] Hearing- or speech-challenged individuals may access this number through TTY by calling the Federal Relay Service at 1-800-877-8399.

What You Can Do Now to Protect Your Family

If you suspect that your house has lead-based paint hazards, you can take some immediate steps to reduce your family's risk:

- If you rent, notify your landlord of peeling or chipping paint.

- Keep painted surfaces clean and free of dust. Clean floors, window frames, window sills, and other surfaces weekly. Use a mop or sponge with warm water and a general all-purpose cleaner. (Remember: never mix ammonia and bleach products together because they can form a dangerous gas.)

- Carefully clean up paint chips immediately without creating dust.

- Thoroughly rinse sponges and mop heads often during cleaning of dirty or dusty areas, and again afterward.

- Wash your hands and your children's hands often, especially before they eat and before nap time and bed time.

- Keep play areas clean. Wash bottles, pacifiers, toys, and stuffed animals regularly.

- Keep children from chewing window sills or other painted surfaces, or eating soil.

- When renovating, repairing, or painting, hire only EPA- or state-approved Lead-Safe Certified renovation firms (see page 12).

- Clean or remove shoes before entering your home to avoid tracking in lead from soil.

- Make sure children avoid fatty (or high fat) foods and eat nutritious meals high in iron and calcium. Children with good diets absorb less lead.

9

Reducing Lead Hazards

Disturbing lead-based paint or removing lead improperly can increase the hazard to your family by spreading even more lead dust around the house.

- In addition to day-to-day cleaning and good nutrition, you can **temporarily** reduce lead-based paint hazards by taking actions, such as repairing damaged painted surfaces and planting grass to cover lead-contaminated soil. These actions are not permanent solutions and will need ongoing attention.

- You can minimize exposure to lead when renovating, repairing, or painting by hiring an EPA- or state-certified renovator who is trained in the use of lead-safe work practices. If you are a do-it-yourselfer, learn how to use lead–safe work practices in your home.

- To remove lead hazards permanently, you should hire a certified lead abatement contractor. Abatement (or permanent hazard elimination) methods include removing, sealing, or enclosing lead-based paint with special materials. Just painting over the hazard with regular paint is not permanent control.

Always use a certified contractor who is trained to address lead hazards safely.

- Hire a Lead-Safe Certified firm (see page 12) to perform renovation, repair, or painting (RRP) projects that disturb painted surfaces.

- To correct lead hazards permanently, hire a certified lead abatement professional. This will ensure your contractor knows how to work safely and has the proper equipment to clean up thoroughly.

Certified contractors will employ qualified workers and follow strict safety rules as set by their state or by the federal government.

10

Reducing Lead Hazards, continued

If your home has had lead abatement work done or if the housing is receiving federal assistance, once the work is completed, dust cleanup activities must be conducted until clearance testing indicates that lead dust levels are below the following levels:

- 40 micrograms per square foot ($\mu g/ft^2$) for floors, including carpeted floors

- 250 $\mu g/ft^2$ for interior windows sills

- 400 $\mu g/ft^2$ for window troughs

For help in locating certified lead abatement professionals in your area, call your state or local agency (see pages 14 and 15), or visit epa.gov/lead, or call 1-800-424-LEAD.

11

Renovating, Remodeling, or Repairing (RRP) a Home with Lead-Based Paint

If you hire a contractor to conduct renovation, repair, or painting (RRP) projects in your pre-1978 home or childcare facility (such as pre-school and kindergarten), your contractor must:

- Be a Lead-Safe Certified firm approved by EPA or an EPA-authorized state program

- Use qualified trained individuals (Lead-Safe Certified renovators) who follow specific lead-safe work practices to prevent lead contamination

- Provide a copy of EPA's lead hazard information document, *The Lead-Safe Certified Guide to Renovate Right*

RRP contractors working in pre-1978 homes and childcare facilities must follow lead-safe work practices that:

- **Contain the work area.** The area must be contained so that dust and debris do not escape from the work area. Warning signs must be put up, and plastic or other impermeable material and tape must be used.

- **Avoid renovation methods that generate large amounts of lead-contaminated dust.** Some methods generate so much lead-contaminated dust that their use is prohibited. They are:

  - Open-flame burning or torching

  - Sanding, grinding, planing, needle gunning, or blasting with power tools and equipment not equipped with a shroud and HEPA vacuum attachment and

  - Using a heat gun at temperatures greater than 1100°F

- **Clean up thoroughly.** The work area should be cleaned up daily. When all the work is done, the area must be cleaned up using special cleaning methods.

- **Dispose of waste properly.** Collect and seal waste in a heavy duty bag or sheeting. When transported, ensure that waste is contained to prevent release of dust and debris.

To learn more about EPA's requirements for RRP projects visit epa.gov/getleadsafe, or read *The Lead-Safe Certified Guide to Renovate Right*.

12

Other Sources of Lead

While paint, dust, and soil are the most common sources of lead, other lead sources also exist:

- **Drinking water.** Your home might have plumbing with lead or lead solder. You cannot see, smell, or taste lead, and boiling your water will not get rid of lead. If you think your plumbing might contain lead:

  - Use only cold water for drinking and cooking.

  - Run water for 15 to 30 seconds before drinking it, especially if you have not used your water for a few hours.

  Call your local health department or water supplier to find out about testing your water, or visit epa.gov/lead for EPA's lead in drinking water information.

- **Lead smelters** or other industries that release lead into the air.

- **Your job.** If you work with lead, you could bring it home on your body or clothes. Shower and change clothes before coming home. Launder your work clothes separately from the rest of your family's clothes.

- **Hobbies** that use lead, such as making pottery or stained glass, or refinishing furniture. Call your local health department for information about hobbies that may use lead.

- Old **toys** and **furniture** may have been painted with lead-containing paint. Older toys and other children's products may have parts that contain lead.[4]

- Food and liquids cooked or stored in **lead crystal** or **lead-glazed pottery or porcelain** may contain lead.

- Folk remedies, such as **"greta"** and **"azarcon,"** used to treat an upset stomach.

---

[4] In 1978, the federal government banned toys, other children's products, and furniture with lead-containing paint (16 CFR 1303). In 2008, the federal government banned lead in most children's products. The federal government currently bans lead in excess of 100 ppm by weight in most children's products (76 FR 44463).

13

For More Information

The National Lead Information Center
Learn how to protect children from lead poisoning and get other information about lead hazards on the Web at epa.gov/lead and hud.gov/lead, or call **1-800-424-LEAD (5323).**

EPA's Safe Drinking Water Hotline
For information about lead in drinking water, call **1-800-426-4791**, or visit epa.gov/lead for information about lead in drinking water.

Consumer Product Safety Commission (CPSC) Hotline
For information on lead in toys and other consumer products, or to report an unsafe consumer product or a product-related injury, call **1-800-638-2772,** or visit CPSC's website at cpsc.gov or saferproducts.gov.

State and Local Health and Environmental Agencies
Some states, tribes, and cities have their own rules related to lead-based paint. Check with your local agency to see which laws apply to you. Most agencies can also provide information on finding a lead abatement firm in your area, and on possible sources of financial aid for reducing lead hazards. Receive up-to-date address and phone information for your state or local contacts on the Web at epa.gov/lead, or contact the National Lead Information Center at **1-800-424-LEAD.**

Hearing- or speech-challenged individuals may access any of the phone numbers in this brochure through TTY by calling the toll-free Federal Relay Service at **1-800-877-8339**.

14

U. S. Environmental Protection Agency (EPA) Regional Offices

The mission of EPA is to protect human health and the environment. Your Regional EPA Office can provide further information regarding regulations and lead protection programs.

Region 1 (Connecticut, Massachusetts, Maine, New Hampshire, Rhode Island, Vermont)

Regional Lead Contact
U.S. EPA Region 1
5 Post Office Square, Suite 100, OES 05-4
Boston, MA 02109-3912
(888) 372-7341

Region 2 (New Jersey, New York, Puerto Rico, Virgin Islands)

Regional Lead Contact
U.S. EPA Region 2
2890 Woodbridge Avenue
Building 205, Mail Stop 225
Edison, NJ 08837-3679
(732) 321-6671

Region 3 (Delaware, Maryland, Pennsylvania, Virginia, DC, West Virginia)

Regional Lead Contact
U.S. EPA Region 3
1650 Arch Street
Philadelphia, PA 19103
(215) 814-2088

Region 4 (Alabama, Florida, Georgia, Kentucky, Mississippi, North Carolina, South Carolina, Tennessee)

Regional Lead Contact
U.S. EPA Region 4
AFC Tower, 12th Floor, Air, Pesticides & Toxics
61 Forsyth Street, SW
Atlanta, GA 30303
(404) 562-8998

Region 5 (Illinois, Indiana, Michigan, Minnesota, Ohio, Wisconsin)

Regional Lead Contact
U.S. EPA Region 5 (DT-8J)
77 West Jackson Boulevard
Chicago, IL 60604-3666
(312) 886-7836

Region 6 (Arkansas, Louisiana, New Mexico, Oklahoma, Texas, and 66 Tribes)

Regional Lead Contact
U.S. EPA Region 6
1445 Ross Avenue, 12th Floor
Dallas, TX 75202-2733
(214) 665-2704

Region 7 (Iowa, Kansas, Missouri, Nebraska)

Regional Lead Contact
U.S. EPA Region 7
11201 Renner Blvd.
WWPD/TOPE
Lenexa, KS 66219
(800) 223-0425

Region 8 (Colorado, Montana, North Dakota, South Dakota, Utah, Wyoming)

Regional Lead Contact
U.S. EPA Region 8
1595 Wynkoop St.
Denver, CO 80202
(303) 312-6966

Region 9 (Arizona, California, Hawaii, Nevada)

Regional Lead Contact
U.S. EPA Region 9 (CMD-4-2)
75 Hawthorne Street
San Francisco, CA 94105
(415) 947-4280

Region 10 (Alaska, Idaho, Oregon, Washington)

Regional Lead Contact
U.S. EPA Region 10
Solid Waste & Toxics Unit (WCM-128)
1200 Sixth Avenue, Suite 900
Seattle, WA 98101
(206) 553-1200

15

Consumer Product Safety Commission (CPSC)

The CPSC protects the public against unreasonable risk of injury from consumer products through education, safety standards activities, and enforcement. Contact CPSC for further information regarding consumer product safety and regulations.

CPSC
4330 East West Highway
Bethesda, MD 20814-4421
1-800-638-2772
cpsc.gov or saferproducts.gov

U. S. Department of Housing and Urban Development (HUD)

HUD's mission is to create strong, sustainable, inclusive communities and quality affordable homes for all. Contact HUD's Office of Healthy Homes and Lead Hazard Control for further information regarding the Lead Safe Housing Rule, which protects families in pre-1978 assisted housing, and for the lead hazard control and research grant programs.

HUD
451 Seventh Street, SW, Room 8236
Washington, DC 20410-3000
(202) 402-7698
hud.gov/offices/lead/

U. S. EPA Washington DC 20460
U. S. CPSC Bethesda MD 20814
U. S. HUD Washington DC 20410

EPA-747-K-12-001
September 2013

16

IMPORTANT!

Lead From Paint, Dust, and Soil in and Around Your Home Can Be Dangerous if Not Managed Properly

- Children under 6 years old are most at risk for lead poisoning in your home.

- Lead exposure can harm young children and babies even before they are born.

- Homes, schools, and child care facilities built before 1978 are likely to contain lead-based paint.

- Even children who seem healthy may have dangerous levels of lead in their bodies.

- Disturbing surfaces with lead-based paint or removing lead-based paint improperly can increase the danger to your family.

- People can get lead into their bodies by breathing or swallowing lead dust, or by eating soil or paint chips containing lead.

- People have many options for reducing lead hazards. Generally, lead-based paint that is in good condition is not a hazard (see page 10).

Property Checklist

Address _____

OUTSIDE:
Type of Exterior _____ Need Paint YES __ NO __
Rotted Wood YES __ NO ___ Where _____
Roof Repair   YES __ NO ___ Where _____ Layers _____
Lawn / Tree Service YES___ NO ___ Where_____
Windows Replace YES ___ NO ___ Where_____
Gutters YES ___ NO ___ Any Other Outside Repairs Needed YES ___ NO___
WHAT _____

FOUNDATION:
Type of Foundation _____ Need Work YES___ NO ___
Clearance ___" inches or more YES ___ NO ___ Type of Piers _____
Drainage Good YES ___ NO ___ Need Fill YES __ NO ___ Where _____
Piers on PADS YES ___ NO ___ Are They Capped YES ___ NO ___
NOTES _____

ELECTRIC:
Breaker Box to CODE YES ___ NO ___ Hooked Up YES ___ NO ___
All Outlets Within 6FT. Of Water Equipped With GFCI YES ___ NO ___
How Old is Electrical System_____ Is Any Electrical Missing YES___ NO ___
Wire Aluminum of Copper & What Shape Is It _____
NOTES _____

PLUMBING / GAS:
Water Hooked Up YES ___ NO ___ Any Leaks YES ___ NO ___
If SO Where _____
Any Sewer Backing Up YES ___ NO ___ If so where _____
Is GAS Hooked Up YES ___ NO ___ Water Heater Electric ___ of Gas ___
Water Heater Properly Vented YES ___ NO ___ Water Heater Work YES ___ NO __
Is The INLET hose to Water Heater Correct Type YES___

INSIDE:
Need Painting YES ___ NO ___ Where _____
Need Sheet Rock YES ___ NO ___ Where _____
All Sinks Work Yes ___ NO ___ If Not What _____
Tubs work YES ___ NO ___ Notes _____ Toilets YES ___ NO ___ Notes _____
Carpet's Good YES ___ NO ___ Vinyl Good YES ___ NO ___
Should We Replace Any YES ___ NO ___ Where _____
NOTES _____

GARAGE:
Need Painting YES ___ NO ___ Need Roof YES ___ NO ___ Layers ___
Electricity YES ___ NO ___ Condition ___ Foundation Condition _____ 1 2 3 Cars
Sheet Rock YES ___ NO ___ Plumbing YES ___ NO ___ Water Supply YES ___ NO ___
NOTES_____
_____
_____

Move In Checklist

Condition of Rental Property Checklist

Instructions: Tenant(s) complete(s) this checklist within three days of moving in and tenant(s) and landlord or manager review property and completed checklist together and mutually agree on the condition of the property upon move-in by signing this form. Each party keeps a copy of signed checklist. Tenant(s) and landlord or manager uses the move-in checklist during the pre-move out inspection and again when determining if any of the tenant's deposit will be retained for cleaning or repairs after move-out. BE SPECIFIC and DETAILED when filling out the checklist.

Tenant Name (Print)_____

Tenant Name (Print)_____

Tenant Name (Print)_____

Tenant Name (Print)_____

Tenant Name (Print)_____

_____
Property Address

_____
Landlord/Manager Name (Print)

ITEM	CONDITION ON ARRIVAL	CONDITION ON DEPARTURE
LIVING ROOM		
Floor & Floor Covering		
Walls & Ceiling		
Door(s)		
Door Lock(s) & Hardware		
Lighting Fixture(s)		
Window(s) & Screen(s)		
Window Covering(s)		
Smoke Alarm		
Carbon Monoxide Alarm		
Fireplace		
KITCHEN		
Floor & Floor Coverings		
Walls & Ceiling		
Door(s)		
Door Lock(s) and Hardware		
Window(s) & Screen(s)		
Window Covering(s)		
Light Fixture(s)		
Cabinets		
Counters		
Stove/Oven/Range Hood		
Refrigerator		
Dishwasher		
Sink(s) & Plumbing		
Garbage Disposal		
Fire Extinguisher		
Other		

CONDITION OF RENTAL PROPERTY CHECKLIST

ITEM	CONDITION ON ARRIVAL	CONDITION ON DEPARTURE
DINING ROOM		
Floor & Floor Covering(s)		
Walls & Celing		
Light Fixture(s)		
Window(s) & Screen(s)		
Window Covering(s)		
Other		
BATHROOM #1		
Floors & Floor Covering(s)		
Walls & Ceilings		
Counters & Surfaces		
Window(s) & Screen(s)		
Window Covering(s)		
Sink & Plumbing		
Bathtub/Shower		
Toilet		
Light Fixture(s)		
Door(s)		
Door Lock(s) & Hardware(s)		
Other		
BATHROOM #2		
Floor & Floor Covering(s)		
Walls & Ceiling		
Counters & Surfaces		
Window(s) & Screen(s)		
Window Covering(s)		
Sink & Plumbing		
Bathtub/Shower		
Toilet		
Light Fixture(s)		
Door(s)		
Door Lock(s) & Hardware(s)		
Other		

Page 2

CONDITION OF RENTAL PROPERTY CHECKLIST

ITEM	CONDITION ON ARRIVAL	CONDITION ON DEPARTURE
BEDROOM #1		
Floor & Floor Covering(s)		
Walls & Ceiling		
Window(s) & Screen(s)		
Window Covering(s)		
Closet(s), including Doors & Tracks		
Lighting Fixture(s)		
Smoke Alarm		
Carbon Monoxide Alarm		
Door(s)		
Door Lock(s) & Hardware		
BEDROOM #2		
Floor & Floor Covering(s)		
Walls & Ceiling		
Window(s) & Screen(s)		
Window Covering(s)		
Closet, including Doors & Tracks		
Lighting Fixtures		
Smoke Alarm		
Carbon Monoxide Alarm		
Door(s)		
Door Lock(s) & Hardware		
BEDROOM #3		
Floor & Floor Covering(s)		
Walls & Ceiling		
Window(s) & Screen(s)		
Window Covering(s)		
Closet, including Doors & Tracks		
Lighting Fixtures		
Smoke Alarm		
Carbon Monoxide Alarm		
Door(s)		
Door Lock(s) & Hardware		
HALL		
Smoke Alarm		
Carbon Monoxide Alarm		

CONDITION OF RENTAL PROPERTY CHECKLIST

ITEM	CONDITION ON ARRIVAL	CONDITION ON DEPARTURE
OTHER		
Heating System		
Air Conditioning		
Stair(s)		
Hallway(s)		
Lawn(s) & Garden(s)		
Patio, Terrace, Deck, etc		
Parking Area(s)		
Other		
Other		
Other		
Other		
# of Keys Received:		

Tenants acknowledge that all smoke alarms, carbon monoxide alarms, and fire extinguishers were tested in their presence and found to be in working order, and that the testing procedure was explained to them. Tenants agree to test all detectors at least once a month and to report any problems to Landlord/Manager in writing.

Comments: _____

_____

_____

_____

_____

_____

_____

_____

MOVE-IN INSPECTION DATE:_____   MOVE-OUT INSPECTION DATE:_____

_____   _____
Owner/Agent Signature   Owner/Agent Signature

_____   _____
Tenant Signature   Tenant Signature

_____   _____
Tenant Signature   Tenant Signature

_____   _____
Tenant Signature   Tenant Signature

_____   _____
Tenant Signature   Tenant Signature

_____   _____
Tenant Signature   Tenant Signature

Home Styles – St Louis Area

Ranch

Split Level

Condo

Townhouse

Slab

Mobile Home

Colonial

Tudor

1.5 Story

Bungalow

Craftsman

Walk-out

Victorian

Queen Anne

Art Deco

Danish/50s Modern

Southwest

Understanding & Improving
YOUR Credit Scores

Why should *You* care about Credit Scores and having a good one? Many people don't. Smart people do. A good credit score will allow you to *choose* who you want to do business with instead of who will do business with you.

With a good credit score you will get much more favorable interest rates on your loan, e.g. mortgages, auto loans, credit cards and more. You'll also get better rates on your insurance premiums, auto, homeowners and renters insurance to name a few. Many employers also check your credit before hiring you for employment.

What are credit scores designed to do? Many will tell you it's your ability to pay back a loan, say if you're a good or bad credit risk or something like that. Credit scores are *actually* a predictor to show the likelihood that a borrower will become 90 days delinquent on an account within the next 24 months.

How do the CRAs (credit reporting agencies) come up with the credit scores? There are a few factors that matter more than others.

35% = Payment History
10% = Types of Credit
10% = Credit Inquiries
15% = Credit History
30% = Amount, i.e. proportion of balance to limits

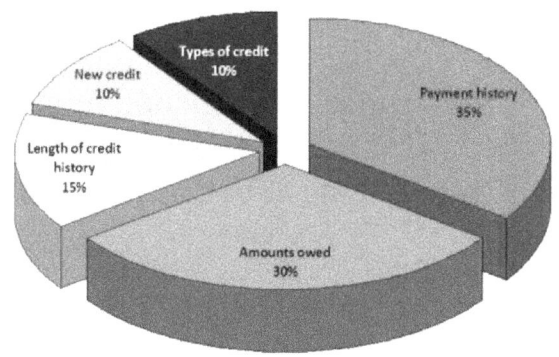

What about those *credit repair* companies? All I can say about *those* companies is to use extreme caution. A lot of them are very confusing. Some lead you to believe that they know some *secret* that is unavailable to you. Not true. There's nothing they can do that you cannot do yourself. Improving your credit score is not brain surgery.

With just a little education you can improve your score. Many of *those companies* make outrageous claims. They say things like, we can remove negative credit from your report or we can improve your score to 720 in 30 days and all kinds of other "guarantees".

The truth is, there are No guarantees when you are attempting to improve your score. In fact, many times your score will *go down* when you wake up the negative sleeping giants that are reporting on your credit report.

Some lenders will require you to pay off old collections before extending you credit. Just by waking this *sleeping dog*, they may update the collection and your credit score will reflect this negativity like it is a new collection. It can be best to pay the collection at closing or get them to remove it from your report altogether when paid. This needs to be in writing.

You can dispute negative credit, collections, judgments, etc. Many times they will be removed. Many times they will not. Anyone that tells you that they *guarantee* these will be removed is either not being truthful or doesn't know what they are talking about. It may be best for you to do a 180 and keep walking.

What about those that say you can set up a whole new credit file with an EIN (employer identification number) or some other way? I have never seen a way to do this. At least, not that I know of *legally.*

The bottom line is there are no magical ways to improve you credit score. There are ways that you can improve your credit score.

Six ways to improve your credit score:

- Pay Your Bills on time
- Don't necessarily close older and/or paid off accounts
- Don't get unnecessary inquiries
- Keep balances in proportion to limits at 30-40% or less
- Dispute incorrect information
- Add a Fraud statement

"Understanding and Improving Credit Scores" can be a very important part of our lives. A little education can go a long way. ☺

To Your Success !!!

John Lee theDealionaire@gmail.com

"Develop an 'Attitude of Gratitude'. Say Thank You to Everyone You Meet for Everything They Do for You."
-Brian Tracy

REAL ESTATE ABBREVIATIONS

APR	Annual Percentage Rate
ARM	Adjustable Rate Mortgage
ARV	After Repair Value
BOM	Bill of Materials
BPO	Broker's Price Opinion
CAP	Capitalization Rate
COM	Comparative Market Analysis
DOM	Days on Market
DSCR	Debt Service Coverage Ratio
DTI	Debt to Income ration
EIN	Employer Identification Number
FDIC	Federal Deposit Insurance Corporation
FMV	Fair Market Value
FHA	Federal Housing Administration
FICO	Fair Isaac Corporation
GIP	Gross Investor Profit
HELOC	Home Equity Line of Credit
HOA	Home Owners Association
HUD	Housing and Urban Development
LRA	Land Reutilization Authority
LTV	Loan To Value
NOI	Net Operating income
MAO	Maximum Allowable Offer
MIP	Mortgage Insurance Premium
MLS	Multiple Listing Service

P&L	Profit and Loss Statement
PITI	Principal, Interest, Taxes, and Insurance
PMI	Private Mortgage Insurance
RCE	Repair Cost Estimate
REIA	Real Estate Investment Association
REO	Real Estate Owned (Bank Owned Properties)
RESPA	Real Estate Settlement Procedures Act
ROI	Return on Investment
SDIRA	Self-Directed Individual Retirement Account
SFR	Single Family Residence
VA	Veterans Administration

"Things Work Out Best for Those Who make the Best of How Things Work Out."
-John Wooden

REAL ESTATE INVESTING STRATEGIES

BRRRR
Buy, Rehab, Rent, Refinance, Repeat. The goal behind a BRRRR strategy is to pull all of the money you put into a property out when you refinance it so that you effectively bought a property for nothing, but still have 25 percent built-in equity to reduce risk.

Buy and Hold / Rentals
Holding rental property for a period of time, during which the property pays for itself through rental income, producing cash to pay all expenses while also producing an annual profit for the owners. These properties can be sold for a profit as equity builds, or held long-term to generate passive income. Most common are single family or 2-4 unit multifamily rental property. Others invest in mobile homes or self-storage units. Rental investors either manage properties themselves or hire a property manager.

Crowdfunding
Relatively new, investors are found online. The SEC allows only accredited investors to invest in individual assets that are crowdfunded.

Flipping
Buy a property, make improvements yourself or with contractors, and sell. Flippers take advantage of inefficiencies in the market, bringing a lot of experience to plan and oversee a project, then selling for (hopefully) a profit.

Notes
The origination of new, or the purchase of existing real estate secured mortgages and/or trust deeds. The terms of a mortgage are detailed in the promissory "note." The real estate is not owned by the note holder: the note holder has a lien position against the real estate. If the borrower breaches the terms of the loan agreement, the lien holder can foreclose upon their interest and acquire title to the property.

Private Lending or Partnering
Instead of being actively involved in house flipping or buying a rental property, you can be a private lender or equity partner. Let other people do all the work involved with finding deals, lining up projects, and filling apartments, but you get to earn some of the profits. All you have to do is vet the investor and underwrite the deals to make sure it makes sense.

Wholesaling
Wholesalers try to find and negotiate really good deals, then sell that contract to a house flipper or landlord. Wholesaling requires an investor to land a deal for cheap and sell that deal for a quick profit. Wholesale property prices are below retail price. If you want access to wholesale deals, you need to get on buyers lists.

REAL ESTATE MATH

ARV Calculation:
Price/Sq. Foot Avg. for the area **X** Subject Property sq. ft.. =
Anticipated ARV

Net operating income (NOI)
NOI= annual income - operating expenses

(Operating Expenses: taxes, insurance, manangement,
maintenance/repairs, utilities) NOT MORTGAGE

Return on Investment (ROI) ROI = NOI ÷ Cash Investment

Cash Flow = NOI - Mortgage

Cash on Cash Return (COC) – (for the 1st year of the
investment)

COC = Cash Flow ÷ Cash In (down payment and closing costs)

Capitalization Rate (Cap Rate) %
Cap Rate = NOI ÷ Purchase Price

Debt Service Coverage Ratio (DSCR)
DCSR = (NOI) ÷ annual mortgage debt (principal + interest)

Maximum Allowable Offer (MAO)
ARV (after repair value)
X .7 or .65 (This multiplier changes based on your market)
- Repairs
- Profit
=Max Offer

A person who won't read has no advantage over one who can't read. – Mark Twain

Real Estate Jargon

Know what you own and know why you own it.
– Peter Lynch

Acceleration Clause
A clause in your mortgage, which allows the lender to demand payment of the outstanding loan balance for various reasons. The most common reasons for accelerating a loan are if the borrower defaults on the loan or transfers title to another individual without informing the lender.

Adjustable Rate Mortgage (ARM)
A mortgage in which the interest changes periodically, according to corresponding fluctuations in an index. All ARMs are tied to indexes.

Adjustment Date
The date the interest rate changes on an adjustable-rate mortgage (ARM).

Amortization
The loan payment consists of a portion which will be applied to pay the accruing interest on a loan, with the remainder being applied to the principal. Over time, the interest portion decreases as the loan balance decreases, and the amount applied to principal increases so that the loan is paid off (amortized) in the specified time.

Amortization Schedule
A table which shows how much of each payment will be applied toward principal and how much toward interest over the life of the loan. It also shows the gradual decrease of the loan balance until it reaches zero.

Annual Percentage Rate (APR)
This is not the note rate on your loan. It is a value created according to a government formula intended to reflect the true annual cost of borrowing, expressed as a percentage. It works sort of like this, but not exactly, so only use this as a guideline: deduct the closing costs from your loan amount, then using your actual loan payment, calculate what the interest rate would be on this amount instead of your actual loan amount. You will come up with a number close to the APR. Because you are using the same payment on a smaller amount, the APR is always higher than the actual not rate on your loan.

Application
The form used to apply for a mortgage loan, containing information about a borrower's income, savings, assets, debts, and more.

Appraisal
A written justification of the price paid for a property, primarily based on an analysis of comparable sales of similar homes nearby.

Appraised Value
An opinion of a property's fair market value, based on an appraiser's knowledge, experience, and analysis of the property. Since an appraisal is based primarily on comparable sales, and the most recent sale is the one on the property in question, the appraisal usually comes out at the purchase price.

Appraiser

An individual qualified by education, training, and experience to estimate the value of real property and personal property. Although some appraisers work directly for mortgage lenders, most are independent.

Appreciation

The increase in the value of a property due to changes in market conditions, inflation, or other causes.

Assessed value

The valuation placed on property by a public tax assessor for purposes of taxation.

Assessment

The placing of a value on property for the purpose of taxation.

Assessor

A public official who establishes the value of a property for taxation purposes.

Asset

Items of value owned by an individual. Assets that can be quickly converted into cash are considered "liquid assets." These include bank accounts, stocks, bonds, mutual funds, and so on. Other assets include real estate, personal property, and debts owed to an individual by others.

Assignment

When ownership of your mortgage is transferred from one company or individual to another, it is called an assignment.

Assignment Fee

Encompasses the transfer of rights held by one party, the assignor, to another party, the assignee. An assignment allows another buyer to take over the buyer's rights. Imagine that one is stepping into the shoes of the Original Purchaser for a **fee** in order to purchase the desired property.

Assumable mortgage

A mortgage that can be assumed by the buyer when a home is sold. Usually, the borrower must "qualify" in order to assume the loan.

Assumption

The term applied when a buyer assumes the seller's mortgage.

Balloon mortgage

A mortgage loan that requires the remaining principal balance be paid at a specific point in time. For example, a loan may be amortized as if it would be paid over a thirty year period, but requires that at the end of the tenth year the entire remaining balance must be paid.

Balloon payment

The final lump sum payment that is due at the termination of a balloon mortgage.

Bankruptcy

By filing in federal bankruptcy court, an individual or individuals can restructure or relieve themselves of debts and liabilities. Bankruptcies are of various types, but the most common for an individual seem to be a "Chapter 7 No Asset" bankruptcy which relieves the borrower of most types of debts. A borrower cannot usually qualify for an "A" paper loan for a period of two years after the bankruptcy has been discharged and requires the re-establishment of an ability to repay debt.

Bill of Sale
A written document that transfers title to personal property. For example, when selling an automobile to acquire funds which will be used as a source of down payment or for closing costs, the lender will usually require the bill of sale (in addition to other items) to help document this source of funds.

Biweekly Mortgage
A mortgage in which you make payments every two weeks instead of once a month. The basic result is that instead of making twelve monthly payments during the year, you make thirteen. The extra payment reduces the principal, substantially reducing the time it takes to pay off a thirty year mortgage. *Note:* there are independent companies that encourage you to set up bi-weekly payment schedules with them on your thirty year mortgage. They charge a set-up fee and a transfer fee for every payment. Your funds are deposited into a trust account from which your monthly payment is then made, and the excess funds then remain in the trust account until enough has accrued to make the additional payment which will then be paid to reduce your principle. You could save money by doing the same thing yourself, plus you have to have faith that once you transfer money to them that they will actually transfer your funds to your lender.

Blanket mortgage

A mortgage covering more than one piece of property. Example: A developer subdivides a tract of land into lots and obtains a blanket mortgage on the whole tract.

Bond

A promise by a third party to repay a principal and interest if another party does not make payment.

Bond Market

Usually refers to the daily buying and selling of thirty year treasury bonds. Lenders follow this market intensely because as the yields of bonds go up and down, fixed rate mortgages do approximately the same thing. The same factors that affect the Treasury Bond market also affect mortgage rates at the same time. That is why rates change daily, and in a volatile market can and do change during the day as well.

Bridge Loan

Not used much anymore, bridge loans are obtained by those who have not yet sold their previous property, but must close on a purchase property. The bridge loan becomes the source of their funds for the down payment. One reason for their fall from favor is that there are more and more second mortgage lenders now that will lend at a high loan to value. In addition, sellers often prefer to accept offers from buyers who have already sold their property.

Broker

Broker has several meanings in different situations. Most Realtors are "agents" who work under a "broker." Some agents are brokers as well, either working form themselves or under another broker. In the mortgage industry, broker usually refers to a company or individual that does not lend the money for the loans themselves, but broker loans to larger lenders or investors. (See the Home Loan Library that discusses the different types of lenders). As a normal definition, a broker is anyone who acts as an agent, bringing two parties together for any type of transaction and earns a fee for doing so.

Broker's Price Opinion

A BPO is the process used by a hired sales agent to determine the potential selling price or estimated **value** of a real estate property. A BPO is popularly used in situations where a financial institution believes the expense and delay of an appraisal is unnecessary.

Buydown

Usually refers to a fixed rate mortgage where the interest rate is "bought down" for a temporary period, usually one to three years. After that time and for the remainder of the term, the borrower's payment is calculated at the note rate. In order to buy down the initial rate for the temporary payment, a lump sum is paid and held in an account used to supplement the borrower's monthly payment. These funds usually come from the seller (or some other source) as a financial incentive to induce someone to buy their property. A "lender funded buydown" is when the lender pays the initial lump sum. They can accomplish this because the note rate on the loan (after the buydown adjustments) will be higher than the current market rate. One reason for doing this is because the borrower may get to "qualify" at the start rate and can qualify for a higher loan amount. Another reason is that a borrower may expect his earnings to go up substantially in the near future, but wants a lower payment right now.

Call Option
Similar to the acceleration clause.

Cap
Adjustable Rate Mortgages have fluctuating interest rates, but those fluctuations are usually limited to a certain amount. Those limitations may apply to how much the loan may adjust over a six-month period, an annual period, and over the life of the loan, and are referred to as "caps." Some ARMs, although they may have a life cap, allow the interest rate to fluctuate freely, but require a certain minimum payment which can change once a year. There is a limit on how much that payment can change each year, and that limit is also referred to as a cap.

Capital gains
Profit earned from the sale of real estate or the amount by which an asset's selling price exceeds its initial purchase price.

Capitalization rate (CAP Rate)
The rate used to determine the present value of property with future earnings.

Carrying Costs
The expenses of maintaining a home or property. For example, mortgage payments, property taxes, insurance, and the expenses of utilities, repairs and upkeep.

Cash Flow
The amount of cash derived over a certain period of time from an income-producing property. Cash receipts minus cash payments over a given period of time. The cash flow should be large enough to pay the expenses of the income-

producing property (mortgage payment, maintenance, utilities, etc.).

Cash Out Refinance
When a borrower refinances his mortgage at a higher amount than the current loan balance with the intention of pulling out money for personal use, it is referred to as a "cash out refinance."

Caveat Emptor
A legal term meaning "let buyer beware". The buyer must examine the property and buy at his/her own risk. Example: A property may be offered in an "as is" condition with no expressed or implied guarantee of quality or condition.

Certificate of Deposit
A time deposit held in a bank which pays a certain amount of interest to the depositor.

Certificate of Deposit Index
One of the indexes used for determining interest rate changes on some adjustable rate mortgages. It is an average of what banks are paying on certificates of deposit.

Certificate of Eligibility
A document issued by the Veterans Administration that certifies a veteran's eligibility for a VA loan.

Certificate of occupancy
Document issued by a local governmental agency that states a property meets the local building standards for occupancy and is in compliance with public health and building codes. This document is normally required by a lender prior to closing the loan.

Certificate of Reasonable Value (CRV)

Once the appraisal has been performed on a property being bought with a VA loan, the Veterans Administration issues a CRV.

Chain of Title

An analysis of the transfers of title to a piece of property over the years.

Clear Title

A title that is free of liens or legal questions as to ownership of the property.

Closing

This has different meanings in different states. In some states a real estate transaction is not consider "closed" until the documents record at the local recorders office. In others, the "closing" is a meeting where all of the documents are signed and money changes hands.

Closing Costs

Closing costs are separated into what are called "non-recurring closing costs" and "pre-paid items." Non-recurring closing costs are any items which are paid just once as a result of buying the property or obtaining a loan. "Pre-paids" are items which recur over time, such as property taxes and homeowners insurance. A lender makes an attempt to estimate the amount of non-recurring closing costs and prepaid items on the Good Faith Estimate which they must issue to the borrower within three days of receiving a home loan application.

Closing Statement

See Settlement Statement.

Cloud on Title

Any conditions revealed by a title search that adversely affect the title to real estate. Usually clouds on title cannot be removed except by deed, release, or court action.

Co-Borrower

An additional individual who is both obligated on the loan and is on title to the property.

Collateral

In a home loan, the property is the collateral. The borrower risks losing the property if the loan is not repaid according to the terms of the mortgage or deed of trust.

Collection

When a borrower falls behind, the lender contacts them in an effort to bring the loan current. The loan goes to "collection." As part of the collection effort, the lender must mail and record certain documents in case they are eventually required to foreclose on the property.

Commission

Most salespeople earn commissions for the work that they do and there are many sales professionals involved in each transaction, including Realtors, loan officers, title representatives, attorneys, escrow representative, and representatives for pest companies, home warranty companies, home inspection companies, insurance agents, and more. The commissions are paid out of the charges paid by the seller or buyer in the purchase transaction. Realtors generally earn the largest commissions, followed by lenders, then the others.

Common Area Assessments
In some areas they are called Homeowners Association Fees. They are charges paid to the Homeowners Association by the owners of the individual units in a condominium or planned unit development (PUD) and are generally used to maintain the property and common areas.

Common Areas
Those portions of a building, land, and amenities owned (or managed) by a planned unit development (PUD) or condominium project's homeowners' association (or a cooperative project's cooperative corporation) that are used by all of the unit owners, who share in the common expenses of their operation and maintenance. Common areas include swimming pools, tennis courts, and other recreational facilities, as well as common corridors of buildings, parking areas, means of ingress and egress, etc.

Common Law
An unwritten body of law based on general custom in England and used to an extent in some states.

Community Property
In some states, especially the southwest, property acquired by a married couple during their marriage is considered to be owned jointly, except under special circumstances. This is an outgrowth of the Spanish and Mexican heritage of the area.

Comparative Market Analysis (CMA)
A comparison of sales prices of similar properties in a given area for the purpose of determining the fair market value of a property. Also referred to as "Comps."

Comparable Sales

Recent sales of similar properties in nearby areas and used to help determine the market value of a property. Also referred to as "comps."

Conditional Commitment

A written document provided by a lender agreeing to make a loan provided certain conditions are met by the borrower prior to closing.

Condominium

A type of ownership in real property where all of the owners own the property, common areas and buildings together, with the exception of the interior of the unit to which they have title. Often mistakenly referred to as a type of construction or development, it actually refers to the type of ownership.

Condominium Conversion

Changing the ownership of an existing building (usually a rental project) to the condominium form of ownership.

Condominium Hotel

A condominium project that has rental or registration desks, short-term occupancy, food and telephone services, and daily cleaning services and that is operated as a commercial hotel even though the units are individually owned. These are often found in resort areas like Hawaii.

Consideration
Anything of value given to induce another to enter into a contract. An earnest money deposit on a sales contract is consideration.

Construction Loan
A short-term, interim loan for financing the cost of construction. The lender makes payments to the builder at periodic intervals as the work progresses.

Contingency
A condition that must be met before a contract is legally binding. For example, home purchasers often include a contingency that specifies that the contract is not binding until the purchaser obtains a satisfactory home inspection report from a qualified home inspector.

Contract
An oral or written agreement to do or not to do a certain thing.

Contract for Deed
A real estate installment selling arrangement where the buyer may occupy the property but the seller retains the title until the agreed upon sales price has been paid. Also known as an installment land contract.

Conventional Mortgage
Refers to home loans other than government loans (VA and FHA).

Convertible ARM
An adjustable-rate mortgage that allows the borrower to change the ARM to a fixed-rate mortgage within a specific time.

Conveyance
The transfer of title of real property from one party to another.

Cooperative (co-op)
A type of multiple ownership in which the residents of a multiunit housing complex own shares in the cooperative corporation that owns the property, giving each resident the right to occupy a specific apartment or unit.

Cost of Funds Index (COFI)
One of the indexes that is used to determine interest rate changes for certain adjustable-rate mortgages. It represents the weighted-average cost of savings, borrowings, and advances of the financial institutions such as banks and savings & loans, in the 11th District of the Federal Home Loan Bank.

Credit
An agreement in which a borrower receives something of value in exchange for a promise to repay the lender at a later date.

Credit History
A record of an individual's repayment of debt. Credit histories are reviewed my mortgage lenders as one of the underwriting criteria in determining credit risk.

Creditor
A person to whom money is owed.

Credit Report
A report of an individual's credit history prepared by a credit bureau and used by a lender in determining a loan applicant's creditworthiness.

Credit Repository
An organization that gathers, records, updates, and stores financial and public records information about the payment records of individuals who are being considered for credit.

Debt
An amount owed to another.

Debt Service Coverage Ratio (DSCR)
A benchmark used by lenders when measuring an income property's ability to cover the mortgage debt after operating expenses is the Debt Service Coverage Ratio (DCSR). The DCSR is calculated by dividing the Net Operating Income (NOI) by the annual mortgage debt (principal + interest).

Debt-to-Income Ratio
The ratio, expressed as a percentage, which results when a borrower's monthly payment obligation on long-term debts is divided by his or her net effective income (FHA/ VA loans) or gross monthly income (conventional loans).

Deed
The legal document conveying title to a property.

Deed In Lieu
Short for "deed in lieu of foreclosure," this conveys title to the lender when the borrower is in default and wants to avoid foreclosure. The lender may or may not cease foreclosure activities if a borrower asks to provide a deed-in-lieu. Regardless of whether the lender accepts the deed-in-lieu, the avoidance and non-repayment of debt will most likely show on a credit history. What a deed-in-lieu may prevent is having the documents preparatory to a foreclosure being recorded and become a matter of public record.

Deed of Trust

Some states, like California, do not record mortgages. Instead, they record a deed of trust which is essentially the same thing.

Default

Failure to make the mortgage payment within a specified period of time. For first mortgages or first trust deeds, if a payment has still not been made within 30 days of the due date, the loan is considered to be in default.

Defective Title

Any recorded instrument that would prevent a grantor/seller from giving a clear title.

Delinquency

Failure to make mortgage payments when mortgage payments are due. For most mortgages, payments are due on the first day of the month. Even though they may not charge a "late fee" for a number of days, the payment is still considered to be late and the loan delinquent. When a loan payment is more than 30 days late, most lenders report the late payment to one or more credit bureaus.

Deposit

A sum of money given in advance of a larger amount being expected in the future. Often called in real estate as an "earnest money deposit."

Depreciation

A decline in the value of property; the opposite of appreciation. Depreciation is also an accounting term which shows the declining monetary value of an asset and is used as an expense to reduce taxable income. Since this is not a true expense where money is actually paid, lenders will add back depreciation expense for self-employed borrowers and count it as income.

Disbursement
(a) The payment of loan money to the borrower usually at or following the closing; (b) Funds paid.

Discount Points
In the mortgage industry, this term is usually used in only in reference to government loans, meaning FHA and VA loans. Discount points refer to any "points" paid in addition to the one percent loan origination fee. A "point" is one percent of the loan amount.

Down Payment
The part of the purchase price of a property that the buyer pays in cash and does not finance with a mortgage.

Due On Sale Provision/Clause
A provision in a mortgage that allows the lender to demand repayment in full if the borrower sells the property that serves as security for the mortgage.

Earnest Money Deposit
A deposit made by the potential home buyer to show that he or she is serious about buying the house.

Easement
A right of way giving persons other than the owner access to or over a property.

Effective Age
An appraiser's estimate of the physical condition of a building. The actual age of a building may be shorter or

longer than its effective age.

Eminent Domain

The right of a government to take private property for public use upon payment of its fair market value. Eminent domain is the basis for condemnation proceedings.

Employer Identification Number (EIN)

Also known as a Federal Tax Identification Number is used to identify a business entity. A new business must file for an identification number with the IRS. An EIN is your permanent number and can be used immediately to open a bank account, for business licenses, and file a tax return by mail.

Encroachment

An improvement that intrudes illegally on another's property.

Encumbrance

Anything that affects or limits the fee simple title to a property, such as mortgages, leases, easements, or restrictions.

Equal Credit Opportunity Act (ECOA)

A federal law that requires lenders and other creditors to make credit equally available without discrimination based on race, color, religion, national origin, age, sex, marital status, or receipt of income from public assistance programs.

Equity

A homeowner's financial interest in a property. Equity is the difference between the fair market value of the property and the amount still owed on its mortgage and other liens.

Equity Partnership
A limited partnership that provides start-up capital to businesses.

Escheat
The reversion of property to the state in the event that the owner dies without leaving a will and has no legal heirs.

Escrow
An item of value, money, or documents deposited with a third party to be delivered upon the fulfillment of a condition. For example, the earnest money deposit is put into escrow until delivered to the seller when the transaction is closed.

Escrow Account
Once you close your purchase transaction, you may have an escrow account or impound account with your lender. This means the amount you pay each month includes an amount above what would be required if you were only paying your principal and interest. The extra money is held in your impound account (escrow account) for the payment of items like property taxes and homeowner's insurance when they come due. The lender pays them with your money instead of you paying them yourself.

Escrow Analysis
Once each year your lender will perform an "escrow analysis" to make sure they are collecting the correct amount of money for the anticipated expenditures.

Escrow Disbursements
The use of escrow funds to pay real estate taxes, hazard insurance, mortgage insurance, and other property expenses as they become due.

Estate

The ownership interest of an individual in real property. The sum total of all the real property and personal property owned by an individual at time of death.

Eviction

The lawful expulsion of an occupant from real property.

Examination of Title

The report on the title of a property from the public records or an abstract of the title.

Exclusive Listing

A written contract that gives a licensed real estate agent the exclusive right to sell a property for a specified time.

Executor

A person named in a will to administer an estate. The court will appoint an administrator if no executor is named. "Executrix" is the feminine form.

Exit Strategy

Money is often made with investment real estate when it is sold. And even if the property is held in order to build equity, a great deal of the profit is made when exiting the investment. Therefore, an exit strategy is essential to making money with real estate.

5 top exit strategies for real estate investors to consider: Wholesale, Flip, Buy and Hold to Build Equity, Seller Financing, Lease Option or Rent-to-Own.

Fair Credit Reporting Act

A consumer protection law that regulates the disclosure of consumer credit reports by consumer/credit reporting agencies and establishes procedures for correcting mistakes on one's credit record.

Fannie Mae/Federal National mortgage Association (FNMA)

A federal organization that purchases loans from lenders and then sells them as FNMA mortgage backed securities.

Farmers Home Administration (FMHA)

An agency, within the U.S. Department of Agriculture, that makes and insures loans for rural housing and farms.

Federal Deposit Insurance Corporation (FDIC)

A government agency that supervises and insures accounts held by lending institutions.

Fee Simple (Fee Absolute or Fee Simple Absolute)

Absolute ownership of real property; owner is entitled to the entire property with unrestricted power of disposition during the owners life and upon his death the property descends to the owner's designated heirs.

Federal Housing Administration (FHA)

A government agency within HUD that administers and insures mortgage loans for private lending agencies.

FHA Loan

This program provides mortgage insurance to protect lenders against the risk of default on loans to qualified buyers. A loan insured by the Federal Housing Administration is open to all qualified home purchasers.

FICO (Fair Isaac Corporation)

The first company to offer a credit-risk model with a **score**. Credit scores are reported by three major credit bureaus, Equifax, Experian and Trans-Union. Scores are not necessarily the same on each bureau's report because each bureau may place a slightly different value on different items. Model Factors: payment history, outstanding debt, length of history, inquiries, types of credit in use. By law, everyone is entitled to receive one free credit report from each of the three major credit bureaus every 12 months.

Fair Market Value (FMV)
The highest price that a buyer, willing but not compelled to buy, would pay, and the lowest a seller, willing but not compelled to sell, would accept.

Fannie Mae (FNMA)
The Federal National Mortgage Association, which is a congressionally chartered, shareholder-owned company that is the nation's largest supplier of home mortgage funds. For a discussion of the roles of Fannie Mae, Freddie Mac (FHLMC), and Ginnie Mae (GNMA), see the Library.

Fannie Mae's Community Home Buyer's Program
An income-based community lending model, under which mortgage insurers and Fannie Mae offer flexible underwriting guidelines to increase a low- or moderate-income family's buying power and to decrease the total amount of cash needed to purchase a home. Borrowers who participate in this model are required to attend pre-purchase home-buyer education sessions.

Federal Housing Administration (FHA)
An agency of the U.S. Department of Housing and Urban Development (HUD). Its main activity is the insuring of residential mortgage loans made by private lenders. The FHA sets standards for construction and underwriting but does not lend money or plan or construct housing.

Fee Simple
The greatest possible interest a person can have in real estate.

Fee Simple Estate
An unconditional, unlimited estate of inheritance that represents the greatest estate and most extensive interest in land that can be enjoyed. It is of perpetual duration. When the real estate is in a condominium project, the unit owner is the exclusive owner only of the air space within his or her portion of the building (the unit) and is an owner in common with respect to the land and other common portions of the property.

FHA Mortgage
A mortgage that is insured by the Federal Housing Administration (FHA). Along with VA loans, an FHA loan will often be referred to as a government loan.

Fiduciary
A company that holds the assets of another party and invests them on behalf of the party.

Finance Charge
Interest charged by a lender.

Financial Reports
Reports such as income statements, cash flows, and balance sheets that are used when documenting the financial aspects of your business.

Firm Commitment
A lender's agreement to make a loan to a specific borrower on a specific property.

First Mortgage
The mortgage that is in first place among any loans recorded against a property. Usually refers to the date in which loans are recorded, but there are exceptions.

Fiscal Year
An accounting period consisting of 12 months.

Fixed Cost
A cost that does not vary with the volume of sales or production.

Fixed Rate Mortgage
A mortgage in which the interest rate does not change during the entire term of the loan.

Fixture
Personal property that becomes real property when attached in a permanent manner to real estate.

Flood Insurance
Insurance that compensates for physical property damage resulting from flooding. It is required for properties located in federally designated flood areas.

Forbearance
A lenders postponement of foreclosure in order to give the borrower time and an opportunity to make up for overdue payments. Also, an agreement for a buyer to temporarily make higher payments in order to satisfy overdue payments.

Foreclosure
The legal process by which a borrower in default under a mortgage is deprived of his or her interest in the mortgaged property. This usually involves a forced sale of the property

at public auction with the proceeds of the sale being applied to the mortgage debt.

Free and Clear
A property that has no liens.

FSBO (For Sale By Owner)
A property for sale that is not listed with a real estate broker and therefore will not be listed on the Multiple Listing Service (MLS).

401(k)/403(b)
An employer-sponsored investment plan that allows individuals to set aside tax-deferred income for retirement or emergency purposes. 401(k) plans are provided by employers that are private corporations. 403(b) plans are provided by employers that are not for profit organizations.

401(k)/403(b) loan
Some administrators of 401(k)/403(b) plans allow for loans against the monies you have accumulated in these plans. Loans against 401K plans are an acceptable source of down payment for most types of loans.

Government Loan (Mortgage)
A mortgage that is insured by the Federal Housing Administration (FHA) or guaranteed by the Department of Veterans Affairs (VA) or the Rural Housing Service (RHS). Mortgages that are not government loans are classified as conventional loans.

Government National Mortgage Association (Ginnie Mae)
A government-owned corporation within the U.S. Department of Housing and Urban Development (HUD).

Created by Congress on September 1, 1968, GNMA performs the same role as Fannie Mae and Freddie Mac in providing funds to lenders for making home loans. The difference is that Ginnie Mae provides funds for government loans (FHA and VA)

Grace Period
The period from the time a payment is due to the point at which a creditor will take legal action.

Grantee
The person to whom an interest in real property is conveyed.

Grantor
The person conveying an interest in real property.

Hard Money Lender - Lenders who use private money to make loans with Borrowers who have trouble getting loans via conventional methods. There is usually a very high interest rate associated with hard money lenders.

Hazard Insurance
Insurance coverage that in the event of physical damage to a property from fire, wind, vandalism, or other hazards.

Home Equity Conversion Mortgage (HECM)
Usually referred to as a reverse annuity mortgage, what makes this type of mortgage unique is that instead of making payments to a lender, the lender makes payments to you. It enables older home owners to convert the equity they have in their homes into cash, usually in the form of monthly payments. Unlike traditional home equity loans, a borrower does not qualify on the basis of income but on the value of his or her home. In addition, the loan does not have to be repaid until the borrower no longer occupies the property.

Home Equity line of Credit (HELOC)
A mortgage loan, usually in second position, that allows the borrower to obtain cash drawn against the equity of his home, up to a predetermined amount.

Home Inspection
A thorough inspection by a professional that evaluates the structural and mechanical condition of a property. A satisfactory home inspection is often included as a contingency by the purchaser.

Homeowners' Association (HOA)
A nonprofit association that manages the common areas of a planned unit development (PUD) or condominium project. In a condominium project, it has no ownership interest in the common elements. In a PUD project, it holds title to the common elements.

Homeowner's Insurance
An insurance policy that combines personal liability insurance and hazard insurance coverage for a dwelling and its contents.

Homeowner's Warranty
A type of insurance often purchased by homebuyers that will cover repairs to certain items, such as heating or air conditioning, should they break down within the coverage period. The buyer often requests the seller to pay for this coverage as a condition of the sale, but either party can pay.

Homestead
Status provided to a homeowner's principal residence in some states that protects the home against certain judgments up to specified amounts.

Homestead exemption

Available in some states - this causes the assessed value of a principal residence to be reduced by the amount of the exemption for the purposes of calculating property tax.

Housing and Urban Development (HUD)

A U.S. government agency established to implement certain federal housing and community development programs.

Housing Choice Voucher

Formerly known as Section Eight, is a rental assistance program funded by the U.S. Department of Housing and Urban Development (HUD). The program allows low-income families, elderly and disabled households to find affordable housing in the private market and receive assistance in paying their monthly rent. Qualified participants receive a voucher and may choose from a variety of housing options, including apartments, duplexes, single-family homes and townhomes where the owner agrees to rent under the program. Rental units must meet minimum standards of health and safety, as determined by HASLC. A housing subsidy is paid to the landlord directly by HASLC on behalf of the participating family. The family then pays the difference between the actual rent charged by the landlord under the Housing Assistance Payment (HAP) contract and the amount subsidized by the program.

HUD Median Income

Median family income for a particular county or metropolitan statistical area (MSA), as estimated by the Department of Housing and Urban Development (HUD).

HUD-1 Settlement Statement

A document that provides an itemized listing of the funds that were paid at closing. Items that appear on the statement include real estate commissions, loan fees, points, and initial escrow (impound) amounts. Each type of expense goes on a specific numbered line on the sheet. The totals at the bottom of the HUD-1 statement define the seller's net proceeds and the buyer's net payment at closing. It is called a HUD1 because the form is printed by the Department of Housing and Urban Development (HUD). The HUD1 statement is also known as the "closing statement" or "settlement sheet."

Improvements

Additions to raw land such as buildings, streets, etc. that add value to the land.

Income Approach

A method used by an appraiser to estimate the value of rental property based on the income it generates over the life of the structure, discounted to determine its present value.

Income Property

Real estate that generates revenue such as rental income.

Ingress and Egress

The right to go in and out over a piece of property but not the right to park on it. See also Easements.

Inspection

An examination of a property or building to determine condition or quality for a particular purpose such as an assessment of structural or termite damage. An inspection may also be used to con rm that the property meets the standards of the contract.

Installment sale
See land contract.

Interest Cap
A limit on the amount that the interest rate for an adjustable rate mortgage can change, regardless of how much the index changes. Most ARMs have a cap on both the amount they can increase and decrease at any periodic adjustment interval, and a life-long cap that limits the amount the interest rate can vary over the life of the loan. The two interest caps are sometimes called a "periodic cap" and a "life cap".

Interest rate
The percentage rate on a principal amount charged by a lender for the use of a sum of money.

Investor
A money source for a lender. Also, one who makes investments.

Joint Tenancy
A form of ownership or taking title to property which means each party owns the whole property and that ownership is not separate. In the event of the death of one party, the survivor owns the property in its entirety.

Joint venture
An agreement between two or more parties that out- lines the financial terms of their interaction, the role and duties of each party, and the intended outcome of the project they will be collectively working on.

Judgment
A decision made by a court of law. In judgments that require the repayment of a debt, the court may place a lien against the debtor's real property as collateral for the judgment's creditor. Alternative spelling is "judgment."

Judicial Foreclosure
A type of foreclosure proceeding used in some states that is handled as a civil lawsuit and conducted entirely under the auspices of a court. Other states use non-judicial foreclosure.

Jumbo Loan
A loan that exceeds Fannie Mae's and Freddie Mac's loan limits, currently at $227,150. Also called a nonconforming loan. Freddie Mac and Fannie Mae loans are referred to as conforming loans.

Junior Lien
A lien which is in a subordinate position to other liens existing on a property.

Junior mortgage
All mortgages/liens subordinate to the rst mortgage.

Land Contract
A real estate installment selling arrangement where-by the buyer may use and occupy land, but ownership of the property is not transferred until all the payments have been made.

Landlord
The owner of real property who rents or leases to another party, called a tenant.

Land trust

A revocable trust agreement usually used in conjunction with a piece of property. The managing party of the agreement, the Trustee, is named in public records while the Beneficiary is not disclosed.

Lease

A written agreement between the property owner and a tenant that stipulates the payment and conditions under which the tenant may possess the real estate for a specified period of time.

Lease Option

An alternative financing option that allows home buyers to lease a home with an option to buy. Each month's rent payment may consist of not only the rent, but an additional amount which can be applied toward the down payment on an already specified price.

Leasehold Estate

A way of holding title to a property wherein the mortgagor does not actually own the property but rather has a recorded long-term lease on it.

Legal Description

A property description, recognized by law, that is sufficient to locate and identify the property without oral testimony.

Legal Rate of Interest

The legal amount a lender can charge a borrower on a loan. This varies from state to state.

Lender

A term which can refer to the institution making the loan or to the individual representing the firm. For example, loan officers are often referred to as "lenders."

Lender seasoning
An ownership time requirement from many lenders that can limit the ability to buy and immediately sell property. The extent to which this is enforced may vary considerably from state to state.

Lessee
A person who leases a property from its owner. (Tenant)

Lessor
A person who rents property to another under a lease. (Landlord)

Liabilities
A person's financial obligations. Liabilities include long-term and short-term debt, as well as any other amounts that are owed to others.

Liability Insurance
Insurance coverage that offers protection against claims alleging that a property owner's negligence or inappropriate action resulted in bodily injury or property damage to another party. It is usually part of a homeowner's insurance policy.

Lien
A legal claim against a property that must be paid off when the property is sold. A mortgage or first trust deed is considered a lien.

Lien Waiver
A document from a contractor, subcontractor, materials supplier, equipment lessor or other party to the construction project (the claimant) stating they have received payment

and waive any future lien rights to the property (of the owner) for the amount paid.

Life Cap
For an adjustable-rate mortgage (ARM), a limit on the amount that the interest rate can increase or decrease over the life of the mortgage.

Limited Power of Attorney
A document giving an investor the ability to control certain or all facets of the sale of a property on behalf of the owner, including the ability to sign on their behalf.

Lis Pendens
Latin term for "Lawsuit Pending"

Line of Credit
An agreement by a commercial bank or other financial institution to extend credit up to a certain amount for a certain time to a specified borrower.

Liquid Asset
A cash asset or an asset that is easily converted into cash.

Loan
A sum of borrowed money (principal) that is generally repaid with interest.

Loan Agreement
The arrangement of payments, conditions, and restrictions signed by the borrower of a loan.

Loan application

A document required by a lender prior to loan approval. The application includes detailed information about the borrower, their finances, and the property.

Loan Officer (LO)

Also referred to by a variety of other terms, such as lender, loan representative, loan "rep," account executive, and others. The loan officer serves several functions and has various responsibilities: they solicit loans, they are the representative of the lending institution, and they represent the borrower to the lending institution.

Loan Origination

How a lender refers to the process of obtaining new loans.

Loan Servicing

After you obtain a loan, the company you make the payments to is "servicing" your loan. They process payments, send statements, manage the escrow/impound account, provide collection efforts on delinquent loans, ensure that insurance and property taxes are made on the property, handle pay-offs and assumptions, and provide a variety of other services

Loan To Value (LTV)

The percentage relationship between the amount of the loan and the appraised value or sales price (whichever is lower).

Lock In

An agreement in which the lender guarantees a specified interest rate for a certain amount of time at a certain cost.

Lock In Period
The time period during which the lender has guaranteed an interest rate to a borrower.

Manufactured Home
Homes built in a factory-controlled environment and that meet strict HUD codes. They are brought to the property site and are assembled there.

Margin
The difference between the interest rate and the index on an adjustable rate mortgage. The margin remains stable over the life of the loan. It is the index which moves up and down.

Maris
Mid America Regional Information Systems (MARIS) administers the Multiple Listing Service (MLS) for the St. Louis, St. Charles County, Jefferson and County Associations and the Franklin County, East Central, South Central and Pulaski County Boards of REALTORS®. The MLS website contains information to help agents achieve the goal of listing and selling real estate.

Market value
The highest price that a buyer would pay and the lowest price a seller would accept on a property.

Maturity
The date on which the principal balance of a loan, bond, or other financial instrument becomes due and payable.

Merged Credit Report
A credit report which reports the raw data pulled from two or more of the major credit repositories. Contrast with a Residential Mortgage Credit Report (RMCR) or a standard

factual credit report.

Modification
Occasionally, a lender will agree to modify the terms of your mortgage without requiring you t refinance. If any changes are made, it is called a modification.

Mortgage
A legal document that pledges a property to the lender as security for payment of a debt. Instead of mortgages, some states use First Trust Deeds.

Mortgage Banker
For a more complete discussion of mortgage banker, see "Types of Lenders." A mortgage banker is generally assumed to originate and fund their own loans, which are then sold on the secondary market, usually to Fannie Mae, Freddie Mac, or Ginnie Mae. However, firms rather loosely apply this term to themselves, whether they are true mortgage bankers or simply mortgage brokers or correspondents.

Mortgage Broker
A mortgage company that originates loans, then places those loans with a variety of other lending institutions with whom they usually have pre-established relationships.

Mortgagee
The lender in a mortgage agreement.

Mortgage Insurance (MI)
Insurance that covers the lender against some of the losses incurred as a result of a default on a home loan. Often mistakenly referred to as PMI, which is actually the name of one of the larger mortgage insurers. Mortgage insurance is

usually required in one form or another on all loans that have a loan-to-value higher than eighty percent. Mortgages above 80% LTV that call themselves "No MI" are usually a made at a higher interest rate. Instead of the borrower paying the mortgage insurance premiums directly, they pay a higher interest rate to the lender, which then pays the mortgage insurance themselves. Also, FHA loans and certain first-time homebuyer programs require mortgage insurance regardless of the loan-to-value.

Mortgage Insurance Premium (MIP)
The amount paid by a mortgagor for mortgage insurance, either to a government agency such as the Federal Housing Administration (FHA) or to a private mortgage insurance (MI) company.

Mortgage Life and Disability Insurance
A type of term life insurance often bought by borrowers. The amount of coverage decreases as the principal balance declines. Some policies also cover the borrower in the event of disability. In the event that the borrower dies while the policy is in force, the debt is automatically satisfied by insurance proceeds. In the case of disability insurance, the insurance will make the mortgage payment for a specified amount of time during the disability. Be careful to read the terms of coverage, however, because often the coverage does not start immediately upon the disability, but after a specified period, sometime forty-five days.

Mortgagor
The borrower in a mortgage agreement.

Motivated Buyer
Any buyer with a strong circumstance or reason to buy.

Motivated seller
Any seller with a strong circumstance or reason to sell.

Multi-Dwelling Units
Properties that provide separate housing units for more than one family, although they secure only a single mortgage.

Multiple Listing Service (MLS)
A group of brokers joined together in a marketing organization for the purpose of pooling their respective listings. In exchange for a potentially larger audience of buyers, the brokers agree to share commissions. The listings are pooled by using a computerized network.

Negative Amortization
Some adjustable rate mortgages allow the interest rate to fluctuate independently of a required minimum payment. If a borrower makes the minimum payment it may not cover all of the interest that would normally be due at the current interest rate. In essence, the borrower is deferring the interest payment, which is why this is called "deferred interest." The deferred interest is added to the balance of the loan and the loan balance grows larger instead of smaller, which is called negative amortization.

Net Operating Income (NOI)
The annual income generated by an income-producing property after taking into account all income collected from operations, and deducting all expenses incurred from operations.

Net Worth
Assets minus total liabilities and debts.

No Cash Out Refinance
A refinance transaction which is not intended to put cash in the hand of the borrower. Instead, the new balance is caculated to cover the balance due on the current loan and any costs associated with obtaining the new mortgage. Often referred to as a "rate and term refinance."

No Cost Loan
Many lenders offer loans that you can obtain at "no cost." You should inquire whether this means there are no "lender" costs associated with the loan, or if it also covers the other costs you would normally have in a purchase or refinance transactions, such as title insurance, escrow fees, settlement fees, appraisal, recording fees, notary fees, and others. These are fees and costs which may be associated with buying a home or obtaining a loan, but not charged directly by the lender. Keep in mind that, like a "no-point" loan, the interest rate will be higher than if you obtain a loan that has costs associated with it.

Note
A legal document that obligates a borrower to repay a mortgage loan at a stated interest rate during a specified period of time.

Note Rate
The interest rate stated on a mortgage note.

No Points Loan
Almost all lenders offer loans at "no points." You will find the interest rate on a "no points" loan is approximately a quarter percent higher than on a loan where you pay one point.

Non-assumption Clause
A statement in a mortgage contract forbidding the assumption of the mortgage without the prior approval of the lender.

Noncompliance
Failure to comply or obey.

Non-Conforming Loan
A loan that does not meet the Freddie Mac or Fannie Mae standards.

Notary Public
One authorized to take acknowledgments of certain types of documents, such as deeds, contracts, and mortgages.

Notice of Default
A formal written notice to a borrower that a default has occurred and that legal action may be taken.

Obligations
Any debts requiring present or future payment.

Offer
An expression of willingness to purchase a property at a specified price.

Offeree
One who receives the offer. When the buyer makes an offer to the seller, the seller is an offeree.

Offeror
One who makes the offer. When the buyer makes an offer to the seller, the buyer is an offeror.

Option

The right to buy a property at a specific price within a specified time period.

Optionee

One who receives or purchases an option.

Optioner

One who gives or sells an option.

Option to Purchase

An agreement giving the right to buy a property at a specific price within a specific time period.

Oral Contract

A verbal agreement. Verbal agreements for the sale or use of real estate are normally unenforceable.

Original Principal Balance

The total amount of principal owed on a mortgage before any payments are made.

Origination Fee

On a government loan the loan origination fee is one percent of the loan amount, but additional points may be charged which are called "discount points." One point equals one percent of the loan amount. On a conventional loan, the loan origination fee refers to the total number of points a borrower pays.

Owner Financing

A property purchase transaction in which the property seller provides all or part of the financing.

Owner Occupant
A tenant of a residence who also owns the property.

Owner of Record
The individual named on a deed that has been recorded at the county recorder's office.

Paper
A mortgage, deed of trust or land contract provided in lieu of cash.

Partial Payment
A payment that is not sufficient to cover the scheduled monthly payment on a mortgage loan. Normally, a lender will not accept a partial payment, but in times of hardship you can make this request of the loan servicing collection department.

Payment Change Date
The date when a new monthly payment amount takes effect on an adjustable-rate mortgage (ARM) or a graduated-payment mortgage (GPM). Generally, the payment change date occurs in the month immediately after the interest rate adjustment date.

Periodic Payment Cap
For an adjustable-rate mortgage where the interest rate and the minimum payment amount fluctuate independently of one another, this is a limit on the amount that payments can increase or decrease during any one adjustment period.

Periodic Rate Cap
For an adjustable-rate mortgage, a limit on the amount that the interest rate can increase or decrease during any one adjustment period, regardless of how high or low the index

might be.

Personal Property
Any property that is not real property.

PITI
This stands for principal, interest, taxes and insurance. If you have an "impounded" loan, then your monthly payment to the lender includes all of these and probably includes mortgage insurance as well. If you do not have an impounded account, then the lender still calculates this amount and uses it as part of determining your debt-to-income ratio.

PITI Reserves
A cash amount that a borrower must have on hand after making a down payment and paying all closing costs for the purchase of a home. The principal, interest, taxes, and insurance (PITI) reserves must equal the amount that the borrower would have to pay for PITI for a predefined number of months.

Planned Unit Development (PUD)
A type of ownership where individuals actually own the building or unit they live in, but common areas are owned jointly with the other members of the development or association. Contrast with condominium, where an individual actually owns the airspace of his unit, but the buildings and common areas are owned jointly with the others in the development or association.

Plat
A plan or map of a specific land area.

Plat Book
A public record containing maps of land, showing the division of the land into streets, blocks, and lots and indicating the measurements of the individual parcels.

Point
A point is 1 percent of the amount of the mortgage.

Portfolio Loan
A loan held (not sold) by banks as an investment.

Power of Attorney
A legal document that authorizes another person to act on one's behalf. A power of attorney can grant complete authority or can be limited to certain acts and/or certain periods of time.

Pre-approval
A loosely used term which is generally taken to mean that a borrower has completed a loan application and provided debt, income, and savings documentation which an underwriter has reviewed and approved. A pre-approval is usually done at a certain loan amount and making assumptions about what the interest rate will actually be at the time the loan is actually made, as well as estimates for the amount that will be paid for property taxes, insurance and others. A pre-approval applies only to the borrower. Once a property is chosen, it must also meet the underwriting guidelines of the lender. Contrast with pre-qualification.

Prepayment
Any amount paid to reduce the principal balance of a loan before the due date. Payment in full on a mortgage that may result from a sale of the property, the owner's decision to pay

off the loan in full, or a foreclosure. In each case, prepayment means payment occurs before the loan has been fully amortized.

Prepayment Penalty
A fee that may be charged to a borrower who pays off a loan before it is due.

Pre-Qualification
This usually refers to the loan officer's written opinion of the ability of a borrower to qualify for a home loan, after the loan officer has made inquiries about debt, income, and savings. The information provided to the loan officer may have been presented verbally or in the form of documentation, and the loan officer may or may not have reviewed a credit report on the borrower.

Prime Rate
The interest rate that banks charge to their preferred customers. Changes in the prime rate are widely publicized in the news media and are used as the indexes in some adjustable rate mortgages, especially home equity lines of credit. Changes in the prime rate do not directly affect other types of mortgages, but the same factors that influence the prime rate also affect the interest rates of mortgage loans.

Principal
The amount borrowed or remaining unpaid. The part of the monthly payment that reduces the remaining balance of a mortgage.

Principal Balance
The outstanding balance of principal on a mortgage. The principal balance does not include interest or any other charges. See remaining balance.

Principal, Interest, Taxes, and Insurance (PITI)

The four components of a monthly mortgage payment on impounded loans. Principal refers to the part of the monthly payment that reduces the remaining balance of the mortgage. Interest is the fee charged for borrowing money. Taxes and insurance refer to the amounts that are paid into an escrow account each month for property taxes and mortgage and hazard insurance.

Private investor

Any non-institutionalized source of funding for a real estate transaction.

Private Mortgage Insurance (PMI, MIP)

Mortgage insurance that is provided by a private mortgage insurance company to protect lenders against loss if a borrower defaults. Most lenders generally require MI for a loan with a loan-to-value (LTV) percentage in excess of 80 percent.

Probate

Court process to establish the validity of the will of a deceased person. Also, the process by which an executor, personal representative or a court-appointed administrator manages and dis- tributes a decedent's property.

Profit and Loss Statement (P&L)

An income statement that shows earnings, expenses, and net profit.

Pro Forma

Projected financial statements based on assumptions.

Promissory Note

A written promise to repay a specified amount over a

specified period of time.

Prorate

To divide proportionately, so as to determine actual amounts owed by the buyer and seller at closing.

Prospectus

A document prepared to outline the terms and potential profitability of a real estate transaction, usually presented to private investors prior to their commitment to a real estate project.

Public Auction

A meeting in an announced public location to sell property to repay a mortgage that is in default.

Planned Unit Development (PUD)

A project or subdivision that includes common property that is owned and maintained by a homeowners' association for the benefit and use of the individual PUD unit owners.

Purchase Agreement

A written contract signed by the buyer and seller stating the terms and conditions under which a property will be sold.

Purchase Money Transaction

The acquisition of property through the payment of money or its equivalent.

Qualifying Ratios

Calculations that are used in determining whether a borrower can qualify for a mortgage. There are two ratios. The "top" or "front" ratio is a calculation of the borrower's monthly housing costs (principle, taxes, insurance, mortgage insurance, homeowner's association fees) as a percentage of monthly income. The "back" or "bottom" ratio includes housing costs as will as all other monthly debt.

Quiet Title (Action)
A court action to establish ownership of property.

Quitclaim Deed
A deed that transfers without warranty whatever interest or title a grantor may have at the time the conveyance is made.

Rate Lock
A commitment issued by a lender to a borrower or other mortgage originator guaranteeing a specified interest rate for a specified period of time at a specific cost.

Real Estate Agent
A person licensed to negotiate and transact the sale of real estate.

Real Estate Broker
A licensed individual who arranges the buying and selling of real estate for a fee. A broker usually owns his/her own real estate company or is in a management position.

Real Estate Settlement Procedures Act (RESPA)
A consumer protection law that requires lenders to give borrowers advance notice of closing costs.

Real Property
Land and appurtenances, including anything of a permanent nature such as structures, trees, minerals, and the interest, benefits, and inherent rights thereof.

Realtor®
A real estate agent, broker or an associate who holds active

membership in a local real estate board that is affiliated with the National Association of Realtors.

Recorder
The public official who keeps records of transactions that affect real property in the area. Sometimes known as a "Registrar of Deeds" or "County Clerk."

Recording
The noting in the registrar's office of the details of a properly executed legal document, such as a deed, a mortgage note, a satisfaction of mortgage, or an extension of mortgage, thereby making it a part of the public record.

Recording Fees
Money paid to the lender for recording a home sale with the local authorities, thereby making it part of the public records.

Red-Lining
Illegal practice of discriminating based on geographic location when providing loans or insurance coverage.

Refinance Transaction
The process of paying off one loan with the proceeds from a new loan using the same property as security.

Remaining Balance
The amount of principal that has not yet been repaid. See principal balance.

Remaining Term
The original amortization term minus the number of payments that have been applied.

Rent Loss Insurance

Insurance that protects a landlord against loss of rent or rental value due to fire or other casualty that renders the leased premises unavailable for use and as a result of which the tenant is excused from paying rent.

Repayment Plan

An arrangement made to repay delinquent installments or advances.

Replacement Reserve Fund

A fund set aside for replacement of common property in a condominium, PUD, or cooperative project -- particularly that which has a short life expectancy, such as carpeting, furniture, etc.

Restrictive Covenants

Private restrictions limiting the use of real property. Restrictive covenants are created by deed and may "run with the land," binding all subsequent purchasers of the land, or may be "personal" and binding only between the original seller and buyer.

Revolving Debt

A credit arrangement, such as a credit card, that allows a customer to borrow against a preapproved line of credit when purchasing goods and services. The borrower is billed for the amount that is actually borrowed plus any interest due.

Return on Investment (ROI)

The income that an investment returns. Profit based on the funds spent to reach it.

Right of First Refusal
A provision in an agreement that requires the owner of a property to give another party the first opportunity to purchase or lease the property before he or she offers it for sale or lease to others.

Right of Ingress or Egress
The right to enter or leave designated premises.

Right of Survivorship
In joint tenancy, the right of survivors to acquire the interest of a deceased joint tenant.

Risk Tolerance
Your comfort level when assessing risk vs. reward. You can take steps to minimize risk in real estate investments.
- Risk Takers –Like speculative investment strategies with attractive potential.
- Moderate Risk Takers – Like speculative types of investments tempered with knowledge of the market demands and application of good investment.
- Risk Averse – Like guaranteed results without risk and are very uncomfortable with taking chances.

Rollover Loan
A loan that is amortized over a long period of time (e.g. 30 years) but the interest rate is fixed for a short period (e.g. 5 years). The loan may be extended or rolled over, at the end of the shorter term, based on the terms of the loan.

Sale Leaseback
A technique in which a seller deeds property to a buyer for a consideration, and the buyer simultaneously leases the property back to the seller.

Second Mortgage
A mortgage that has a lien position subordinate to the first mortgage.

Secondary Market
The buying and selling of existing mortgages, usually as part of a "pool" of mortgages.

Section 1031
The section of the IRS code that deals with tax deferred exchanges of certain property. General rules for tax free exchanges are that the properties must be: exchanged, similar, and used for business or as an investment.

Section 8 Housing
Privately owned rental units participating in the low-income rental assistance program sponsored by HUD. Landlords receive subsidies on behalf of qualified low-income tenants, allowing the tenants to pay a limited proportion of their incomes toward the rent.

Secured Loan
A loan that is backed by collateral.

Security
The property that will be pledged as collateral for a loan.

Seller Carry Back
An agreement in which the owner of a property provides financing, often in combination with an assumable mortgage.

Servicer
An organization that collects principal and interest payments from borrowers and manages borrowers' escrow accounts. The servicer often services mortgages that have been

purchased by an investor in the secondary mortgage market.

Servicing
The collection of mortgage payments from borrowers and related responsibilities of a loan servicer.

Settlement Statement
See HUD1 Settlement Statement

Simple Interest
Interest that is paid on the loan principal.

Sheriff's Deed
A deed given at the sheriff's sale in the foreclosure of a mortgage.

Single Family Residence (SFR)
A general term originally used to distinguish a house designed for use by one family from an apartment house. More recently, this term has also been used to distinguish a house with no common area from a planned development or condominium.

Special Warranty Deed
The grantor does not warrant against title defects arising from conditions that existed before he/she owned the property. The seller warrants that he/she has done nothing to impair title.

Subdivision
A housing development that is created by dividing a tract of land into individual lots for sale or lease.

Subordinate Financing
Any mortgage or other lien that has a priority that is lower

than that of the first mortgage.

Substitution of Liability
A buyer's assumption of responsibility for an assumable loan.

Survey
A drawing or map showing the precise legal boundaries of a property, the location of improvements, easements, rights of way, encroachments, and other physical features.

Sweat Equity
Contribution to the construction or rehabilitation of a property in the form of labor or services rather than cash.

Tax Lien
A lien placed on a property for nonpayment of taxes

Tax Sale
Public sale of a property at an auction by a government authority as a result of non-payment of property taxes.

Tenancy in Common
As opposed to joint tenancy, when there are two or more individuals on title to a piece of property, this type of ownership does not pass ownership to the others in the event of death.

Third Party Origination
A process by which a lender uses another party to completely or partially originate, process, underwrite, close, fund, or package the mortgages it plans to deliver to the secondary mortgage market.

Time is of the Essence
Legal phrase in a contract requiring that all references to specific dates and times in the contract be interpreted exactly.

Title
A legal document evidencing a person's right to or ownership of a property.

Title Company
A company that specializes in examining and insuring titles to real estate.

Title Insurance
Insurance that protects the lender (lender's policy) or the buyer (owner's policy) against loss arising from disputes over ownership of a property.

Title Report
A document indicating the current state of title. The report includes information on the current ownership, outstanding deeds of trust or mortgages, liens, easements, covenants, restrictions, and any defects.

Title Search
A check of the title records to ensure that the seller is the legal owner of the property and that there are no liens or other claims outstanding.

Tract
A parcel of land generally held for subdividing.

Transfer of Ownership
Any means by which the ownership of a property changes hands. Lenders consider all of the following situations to be a transfer of ownership: the purchase of a property "subject to" the mortgage, the assumption of the mortgage debt by the property purchaser, and any exchange of possession of the property under a land sales contract or any other land trust device.

Transfer Tax
State or local tax payable when title passes from one owner to another.

Treasury Index
An index that is used to determine interest rate changes for certain adjustable-rate mortgage (ARM) plans. It is based on the results of auctions that the U.S. Treasury holds for its Treasury bills and securities or is derived from the U.S. Treasury's daily yield curve, which is based on the closing market bid yields on actively traded Treasury securities in the over-the-counter market.

Trustee - A party who is given legal responsibility via a Deed of Trust to hold property in the best interest of or "for the benefit of" another. The trustee is one placed in a position of responsibility for another, a responsibility enforceable in a court of law.

Truth-in-Lending
A federal law that requires lenders to fully disclose, in writing, the terms and conditions of a mortgage, including the annual percentage rate (APR) and other charges.

Two Step Mortgage
An adjustable-rate mortgage (ARM) that has one interest rate for the first five or seven years of its mortgage term and a different interest rate for the remainder of the amortization term.

Two to Four Family Property
A property that consists of a structure that provides living space (dwelling units) for two to four families, although ownership of the structure is evidenced by a single deed.

Underwriting
The decision whether to make a loan to a potential home buyer based on credit, income, employment history, assets, etc.

Unencumbered Property
Real estate with free and clear title.

Unimproved Property
Land that has received no improvements.

VA Mortgage
A mortgage that is guaranteed by the Department of Veterans Affairs (VA).

Valuation
An estimation of value of a property, as determined by various factors.

Vested
Having the right to use a portion of a fund such as an individual retirement fund. For example, individuals who are 100 percent vested can withdraw all of the funds that are set-aside for them in a retirement fund. However, taxes may

be due on any funds that are actually withdrawn.

Veterans Administration (VA)

An agency of the federal government that guarantees residential mortgages made to eligible veterans of the military services. The guarantee protects the lender against loss and thus encourages lenders to make mortgages to veterans.

Waiver

The voluntary renunciation, abandonment, or surrender of some claim, right, or privilege.

Warranty Deed

A deed, which guarantees the transfer of title from the seller to the buyer.

Wholesaling

Wholesaling real estate provides an opportunity for someone to build income with little capital or credit. A wholesaler puts property (normally distressed property) under contract and assigns or resells the property to another investor. The investors a wholesaler sells to either use cash, lines of credit, or hard money loans. This allows quick closings on properties that sometimes need extensive repairs. Wholesaling does not require a real estate license. A license is not required to buy or sell any property that you have an equitable interest in. That interest can be a contractual interest (you have the property under contract) or you actually own or have title to the property.

Wraparound mortgage

A seller created mortgage that includes the remaining amount on a current mortgage AND any remaining amount to reach the agreed upon purchase price. The new mortgage "wraps around" the current mortgage. The seller is still responsible for the 1st mortgage. By making the needed monthly payments on the wrap around mortgage, the buyer will satisfy the terms of the mortgage held by the bank.

Yield spread
A rebate to a mortgage broker from the lending institution that purchases the loan on the open market. The yield spread is usually determined by the difference between the interest rate on the issued loan and the current prime rate.

Zoning
The process of determining what, if any, types of property may be placed in a particular land area. Common zoning distinctions include: residential, commercial, industrial, and agricultural. These zoning ordinances are normally enforced by the city or the county.

ST. LOUIS
REAL ESTATE
INVESTORS
ASSOCIATION
TM

STLREIA Membership
Has Its Privileges

Stay Current www.STLREIA.com

Vendors

We at STLREIA have many great vendors that support our efforts. For a list of our vendors or to find out about becoming a select vendor, go to our website www.STLREIA.com

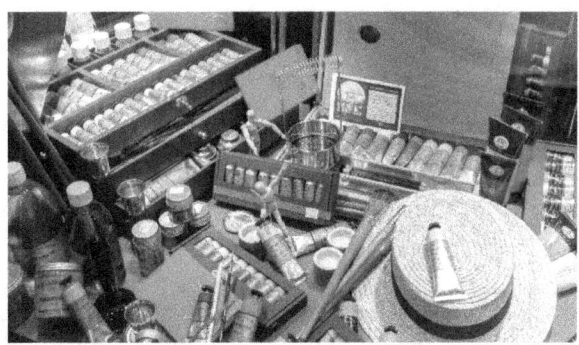

When you invest. You are buying a day that you don't have to work.
-Aya Laraya

Real Estate Websites

www.Auction.com

www.biggerpockets.com

www.blackmold.awardspace.com

www.Crimerates.com

www.Crimereports.com

www.Cyberhomes.com

www.epa.gov/asbestos

www.epa.gov/lead

www.epa.gov/radon

www.fdic.gov

www.greatschools.org

www.gsa.gov

www.haslc.com

www.HomePath.com

www.HomeStagingResource.com

www.HomeSteps.com

www.HousingPredictor.com

www.Hubzu.com

www.HudHomeStore.com

www.justice.gov

www.nextstagefurniture.com

www.Pacer.gov

www.PropertyRadar.com

www.RealEstateABC.com

www.Realtor.com

www.RealtyTrac.com

www.REIblackbook.com

www.Recycler.com

www.resales.usda.gov

www.Schooldigger.com

www.selecthomestager.com

www.Stlouis-mo.gov

www.STLREIA.com

www.Treasury.gov

www.Trulia.com

www.Zillow.com

www.Zbuyer.com

You cannot afford to live in potential for the rest of your life, at some point, you have to unleash the potential and make your move.
-Eric Thomas

Look What Others are Saying About STLREIA!!!

We don't have to be smarter than the rest. We have to be more disciplined than the rest. – Warren Buffett

"This association is a ready source of knowledge.
The newsletter gets my undivided attention as I read about what others are doing to enhance their real state holdings.
The monthly meetings offer time with other investors.
The speakers are experts in their fields. I do not do my own work, but I learn what to look for when hiring workers.
The monthly lunch is another opportunity to visit with investors and exchange ideas.
The web site shows events, articles and advice handling real estate issues to keep me focused on being a successful investor.
Clearly the mission of the association is to be helpful to real estate investors. Because I thankfully accept all the help that I can get I am most grateful for all of you and all the association offers me. Thank you.

"—Ruth Hollander, **STLREIA Long Term Member, Investor**

" STLREIA is my reason I have invested in Real Estate for over 30 years. With negative feed back from my co-workers, landlord images in the media, and problem tenants I've dealt with I probably would have quit. STLREIA gives me a dose of good information with others speaking positively about real estate investing. This keeps me energized and moving forward. Seeking advice from more experienced investors in the group, I also find myself giving advice to less experienced investors. My association with STLREIA a satisfying experience for me."

-Lloyd Alinder, STLREIA Member, Investor, Landlord

"STLREIA is a place I can trust to provide quality education, networking and other resources to boost my potential as an investor. This is a local resource filled with local knowledge which means I can take the information I get from the club's events and apply it directly to my work as quickly as the next day."

—Laura Lenington, STLREIA Member

"I've been to hundreds of real estate associations, seminars and trainings from some of the best trainers on the planet. STLREIA provides a level of value to their members second to none. No question, it's the best investment any real estate entrepreneur can make in their future. If you're the kind of person that wants to be successful in real estate, STLREIA is for *You!*"

—John Lee, STLREIA Member, Investor, Author of best-selling books including "Secrets of a Deal'ionaire", "Landlord Pennies to Banker Dollars", "Secrets THOSE Credit Doctors Don't Want *YOU* to Know", "Secrets to Start Wholesaling Real Estate Today", "Secrets to Winning with Failed Real Estate Deals."

In the real estate business, you learn more about people and you learn more about community issues, you learn more about life, you learn more about the impact of government, probably than any other profession that I know of.
-Jhonny Isakson

FREE Stuff for You!

How to Get Rich in St. Louis Real Estate

What You Need to Know, Get, and Do to Build a Wildly Successful Real Estate Investing Business Starting from Scratch

By Vena Jones-Cox
Author, Lecturer, Real Estate Goddess
TheRealEstateGoddess.com

Go to Our website for *Your Free* copy:
www.STLREIA.com

More FREE Stuff for *You*!

Request Your electronic copy:
theDealionaire@gmail.com

More FREE Stuff for You!

Request Your electronic copy:
theDealionaire@gmail.com

More FREE Stuff for You!

Request Your electronic copy:
theDealionaire@gmail.com

> ## *Bonus Tip: Join STLREIA to Get the Positive Feedback You Need.*
>
> It's not enough to avoid the nay-sayers: you have to have yay-sayers in your life, too! No matter how long you've been investing in real estate or how many successes you've had, it's still awesome to get together with a group of like-minded people to get the support, encouragement, and congratulations you need to get through the discouraging times and celebrate the wins.

Imagine Your Life Is Perfect in Every Respect; What Would It Look Like?"
–Brian Tracy

To All Our Valued STLREIA Members,

Just a quick note to say that you are very much appreciated in our community. There are many choices in REI groups, and I feel that we have chosen the right one.

I have had memberships in many real estate investment organizations and education groups. The very first thing to consider when joining a group is the groups motivation. What is their agenda?

Here's an excerpt from my latest book *Secrets to Winning with Failed Real Estate Deals.*

Know who you are learning from

We have access to many books and videos at little or no cost. Just be aware of where and who you are getting your education from.

A good start is by looking into your local REIA group. That's Real Estate Investing Associations. REIA groups can be found in just about every area of the country. The groups are usually attended by like-minded people who have similar mind sets.

REIAs are a great place to network. They also can be really good places to meet people who have properties to sell, who are looking to buy, or who can help out with some of the things you are looking for with your deals. Things like finding good service and repair people.

There's a huge difference in groups these days, so you should take some time to be sure you are aware of what you are getting into. Be sure to find out the motive that is behind the group you are joining.

There are *not-for-profit* groups like the one I attend. Our board consist entirely of unpaid volunteers. Our group is more about education than most of the other groups that are around.

There are also *for-profit* REIA groups, which include most of the groups that are out there these days. Of course, there's nothing wrong with making a profit. We all need to make money; that's why most of us got into real estate investing to begin with.

(Some of us that have been forced into this arena for other reasons. That's another story. I get into some of this in my book Secrets to Start Wholesaling Real Estate Today.)

There are usually two motivating factors for the for-profit REIAs: selling programs and selling properties.

Many for-profit REIA's are selling you a program or a mentorship. That's okay if you want to speed up your learning process. Many are very good. Some, however, are not.

Just be aware of what you are getting into. Programs and courses can cost anywhere from a couple hundred dollars to tens of thousands of dollars!

Many of these same groups will have fairly new investors giving testimonials—someone who just shelled out $40,000 or $50,000 for their group mentorship program less than a year ago. Listen carefully to these *new* investors.

Many of the testimonials are truly inspiring. These new investors are inspired by the fact that they are going to be able to quit their jobs. They are going to be *rich.* Their motivation has not worn off because they have never dealt with a deal that has failed—at least, not yet.

There is no *get-rich-quick* program in life, and this is especially true in real estate. If someone tells you that there is, they are either lying or they are involved in something illegal. Be extremely skeptical.

Most of the time, these new investors will be telling you about their early successes. Their stories usually revolve around the first deal they did four months ago or so. It may be a story about a four-family rental that will *someday soon* provide them with hundreds of dollars per month in passive income.

Sometimes they will tell you about this great deal they got that provided them with *instant* equity in amounts of tens of thousands of dollars. Many times, this great deal was found for them by their *mentor* or one of their cronies. Are these people making a killing on the backs of new unsuspecting investors? Perhaps.

Before you shell out thousands of dollars to a Guru or a False Profit, talk to someone who they have mentored who has been in the business for a few years. Better yet, see if you can find someone for whom their program or mentorship *didn't* work, someone who spent lots of money with little results. That's where you will get some of the truth about the value of their program.

There are other for-profit REIAs that are motivated by selling you their properties. While some of these *can* be good deals, many of these properties are losers that they have been unable to sell elsewhere.

They will tell you things like, "These properties are not listed on the MLS. This is a wholesale deal!" This may be true. But many of these deals simply cannot be sold as retail properties or on places like the MLS because of their condition.

These properties are often in too bad of shape to sell as retail properties. Also, the sellers may have already attempted to sell them to their network of experienced wholesaling friends with no success.

Most of the time, if it's truly a good deal, you will not be the first to hear about it. Many of the real estate investors who have been around a while have a list of people who they know will jump on screaming good deals, and they offer them to those people first.

There are still other for-profit REIA groups that fill their time with informercials for their sponsors. Many groups thrive on the money the sponsors provide and promote them shamelessly as an additional income source.

That said, the REIA sponsors are not all bad. They can be a great place to find vendors for your investments.

Most of the REIA groups vet their sponsors. Some do not. I recommend doing your own due diligence on all of those you do business with. I recommend due diligence with your education as. Educate yourself *before* getting educated.

You must first learn, and then do (take action). The best learning is in the doing. We learn much more from our mistakes than our successes.

For a FREE copy of my book *Secrets to Winning with Failed Real Estate Deals* send request to theDealionaire@gmail.com

John Lee
STLREIA
Program Coordinator

Secrets of a Deal'ionaire Podcast for RE Investors that Does Not *Break-the-Bank*

"Today Accomplishments Were Yesterday's Impossibilities."
-Robert H. Schuller

Resource Guide

A Special *Thanks* to our **Contributors** who include (and are not necessarily limited to):

- Lloyd Alinder
- Robert G. Allen
- Napoleon Hill
- Jim & Pat Heisserer
- Ruth Hollander
- Vena Jones-Cox
- Current & Past Members

Resource Guide created by *John Lee* 2014-2021 for STLREIA

www.ingramcontent.com/pod-product-compliance
Lightning Source LLC
Chambersburg PA
CBHW080831220526
45467CB00008B/2255